The Kitchen Garden

FIEKE HOOGVELT

 **REBO** PRODUCTIONS

For Bernadette and Ankie

© 1997 Rebo Productions, Lisse

© 1998 Published by Rebo Productions Ltd.

Text: Fieke Hoogvelt

Cover design and layout: Ton Wienbelt, Den Haag, the Netherlands

Editing and production: TextCase, Groningen, The Netherlands

Typesetting: Hof&Land Typografie, Maarssen, the Netherlands

ISBN 1 901094 499

Contents

Foreword

Don't ask me if it is truly worth all the blood, sweat and tears to grow your own vegetables and compete with all those little pests that put up such a fight.

It is difficult to give an honest answer to that question. After all, if you add up everything involved, from the cost of seed and manuring to the preserving pans and the freezer, it's cheaper to go and buy a pound of beans from the greengrocer. Of course – and most importantly – it's great fun being creative in your kitchen garden. And there is no argument about that – after all you are producing your own food. You know exactly how healthy the fruit and vegetables are when you eat them.

Sometimes gardening seems to be a game – a constant battle to outwit the birds, pests and diseases.

And when you do manage to achieve a shaky biological equilibrium, it is like a juggling act to keep it up.

What a wonderful hobby – it does not pollute the environment, and although it's hard work it can still be relaxing. What could be better than giving someone a box of strawberries, scarcely concealing your pride because "you have piles of them".

Of course it is best when everything goes well, and you need a certain basic knowledge to achieve that. You can prevent a lot of problems if you know beforehand that growing cauliflowers on an acid, sandy soil is asking for trouble. And if you know simple ways of improving your soil you can remove a number of stumbling blocks.

With "The Kitchen Garden" as your guide there is no doubt that your organic fruit and vegetable garden will be a healthy and successful one.

Fieke Hoogvelt

Soil, the basis of your kitchen garden

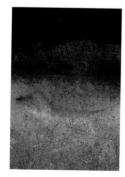

Before you start sowing and planting in your kitchen garden, you must begin by turning your attention to the soil.

The soil provides an anchor for the roots of plants and also acts as a (colourful) background and base for your vegetables. But that is not its only purpose!

The soil has various properties which are vitally important when it comes to the question of whether anything will grow there, what will grow there, and what the results will be. Al-though the words "soil" and "ground" have different meanings in the literature, the difference is not always very clear in practice.

Soil types   The garden mostly consists of soil, but what kind of soil?

The various types of soil in the United Kingdom have been formed over the centuries. The impact of glacial detritus, sand, shells, weathered rocks and deposits of different thicknesses in different places have ensured that the composition of the soil varies widely in this country.

We will begin by looking at the major soil types which are important in the kitchen garden.

Sandy soil   Sand is weathered granite. The remaining quartz is crushed into sand grains, which vary in size from 0.05 to 2 millimetres. Water drains away quickly through the gaps between the large grains and it is difficult to draw up water from the subsoil. The larger the sand grains

Chalky soil can be recognised by a darker layer of organic and mineral components.

Above left: Open podzoi soil with a covering of sand on boulder clay. There is a layer of dissolved nutrients immediately below the surface. Iron (orange), in particular, is suspended at the next level down. This creates an impermeable layer through which water cannot pass. The result is very boggy topsoil.

The beds in this kitchen garden on sandy soil have been raised before sowing and planting.

are, the dryer the garden will be. Fortunately you can improve sandy soil by adding clay, in the form of clay minerals (bentonite or montmorillonite), and organic material.

Soil which is pure sand is not suitable for a (kitchen) garden because it contains no nutrients.

The same garden a few months later... the raised beds have completely collapsed and settled, and the vegetables are extra dry.

Clay soil Clay is also powdered stone, but its origins are completely different from that of sand. In contrast to the quartz in sandy soil, the weathered stone from which clay is made also contains minerals which serve as food for the plants. Since this weathering process is still going on, the nutrients are continually being released. Clay grains are much smaller than sand grains and water does not soak through their very small pores easily.

Clay soils therefore hold water very well, but they do not let much water through. When clay soil does dry out, the underground water takes a long time to rise from the subsoil. Dry clay soil hardens and starts to crack up, while wet clay soil is more susceptible to compacting, because the gaps between the fine clay particles are blocked by the rain. Clay soil is rich in nutrients by nature.

Peat Peat mostly consists of decayed plants. We make a distinction between high moorland peat (which originates from decaying plants above the waterline) and low marsh peat (which comes from plants below water level). Peat retains water very well but also lets it through. Peat which is found high above the level of the water table continues to decompose and settle. Plants grow very fast on this type of soil, but they are not very firm. Using basalt or rock meal causes stronger growth, so that the products can be retained for longer. You can only grow shallow-rooted plants on peat because the water table is usually high.

Since the soil is porous and holds a lot of water, it tends to freeze quickly – with all the consequences of this. This soil type is, therefore, very sensitive to late night frosts.

Sandy clay Sandy clay, also known as light clay soil, is a mixture of clay and not very fine sand, and the proportions dictate the qualities of the soil. The main characteristics of sandy clay are that it is usually productive, easy to work, holds water and has good drainage.

Willowherbs prefer acid soil. You can also get rid of weeds which thrive in acid soil by adding chalk to the soil in autumn.

Loam Loam is the name given to a type of soil which contains both clay particles and exceedingly fine sand grains (0.002-0.050 mm in diameter). If we compare loam with clay, loam is stiffer, less well drained and also less fertile because of the large amount of extremely fine sand. River loam is somewhere in the middle of a scale between the two extremes of sand and clay.

Weeds tell a lot about the soil type. The presence of sorrel indicates a high level of acidity in the soil.

Clay soil cracks and shrinks in dry conditions.

Having read this summary you will probably recognise characteristics of several of these soil types in your own garden. That makes sense, since in practice these soil types are usually mixed.

The structure The soil structure is the way the various components in the soil such as soil particles, water and air, are linked together. What is the ratio between these components? The soil life, the proportion of organic material and the chemical properties of the soil continually affect its structure.

The structure is said to be less good if a lot of puddles remain on the ground for a long time after a shower. It may be that the soil is not well drained, but it can also be a sign that there is an impermeable layer in the soil.

On sandy soils such an impervious layer could be a seam of iron, or iron pan, while on peat it could be a layer of wet clay breaking the continuity between the topsoil and the subsoil. In new housing estates, the problem could be that clay soil heavily compacted by vehicles is covered with a layer of garden soil, but of course the layer of cement where the cement mixer was situated is not conducive to a good structure either.

Persicaria grows in dry soil which is lacking in humus. You can get rid of this weed by improving the soil with compost and organic manure.

Stinging nettles indicate that there is a lot of nitrogen in the ground.

There is also something wrong with the structure if the soil blows away in a strong wind. It may be that the ground does not absorb water after a dry period, but it can also be an indication that a hard crust has formed on the surface.

It should be clear that in order to get a good soil structure, impervious layers must be perforated. Unfortunately that is not always easy to do. Many other soil problems can be cleared up simply by providing a constant supply of humus.

Humus

Humus is the name given to all animal and plant remains and products (including the bodies and manure of animals). It is also called organic material. Plant and animal remains – such as leaves, stalks, wood, sawdust roots, dead animals and smaller organisms such as fungi and bacteria – provide dark-brown carbon after a lengthy process of "combustion" or conversion. In addition, all kinds of materials are released which the plants need in order to live. This organic material (or humus) forms a supply of food in the soil, a kind of buffer in which nutrients are stored. Many tiny invisible creatures, micro-organisms and plants all feed on these nutrients.

The nice thing is that this humus has a cohesive effect on sandy soil, which can therefore hold water better. Humus also works magic on clay and light clay soils: the humus forces the clay soil apart, which

TIP

Vertical drainage: an impermeable layer can be penetrated by boring holes at 3 metre intervals using a soil drill 6 cm in diameter. Fill the holes with gravel or clay pellets up to 25 cm below ground level. Top up the remaining 25 cm with garden soil. The excess water can now soak away underground through these holes.

Vertical drainage: you must stand right behind the soil drill to apply the most power.

Drill the hole using a twisting motion to lift up the soil including the hard layer.

After the hard layer is drilled through, fill the hole with clay pellets or gravel.

Fill in the hole up to 25 cm below the soil surface.

Fill the rest of the hole with garden soil (from the top layer).

loosens the soil – with all the resulting advantages. Humus is darker in colour, so soil containing a lot of humus also tends to be darker. The result is that the soil can absorb more heat from the sun, which has a favourable effect on growth in spring and autumn.

Since the stock of nutrients is constantly shrinking, you must always be replacing this temporary humus. This allows you to ensure that the humus will have a lasting, rather than only a temporary, effect on the soil.

Soil life – differs per layer

Soil life, such as mice, moles, snails, earthworms, mites, insects and their larvae, fungi (toadstools!) and bacteria clear away all plant and animal waste. They break up organic material gradually – that waste is their food.

The sifted compost applied for growing is kept in the topmost layer of soil. The soil will therefore be darker in colour and retain moisture, the sun's heat and nutrients better.

The soil organisms which mainly eat fresh organic material live on and in the top layer of the soil. These organisms need oxygen to work and are, therefore, called aerobic organisms. The material is broken down by their grinding, gnawing or shredding processes and sinks some distance into the soil. Other creatures and bacteria live lower down in anaerobic conditions, eating the wastes from the group above and converting them further. The excrement from this group feeds another group still lower down. Eventually the result is nutrients for the plant. All intermediate stages (excrement) consist of

TIP

Don't throw away a leaking bucket or watering can. These can come in very handy in sandy, well-drained soils when you have to replant something in the "wrong" season. Put the slowly leaking watering can or bucket next to the replanted plant which has to take root. It will do better as a result.

gluey substances which stick the soil particles together, resulting in crumbly, humus-rich soil.

The bacteria and fungi which live in the low-oxygen region of the soil are literally shocked to death if they are brought to the surface, possibly by digging. Conversely, scavenger beetles, slugs and snails die at a depth of 20 cm due to lack of oxygen. It is, therefore, recommended that the soil layers should be kept at their respective levels when working the soil.

Water and air   It is not very surprising that water should be essential for all life on earth because many organisms consist mainly of water. Plants themselves are made up of sixty to ninety percent water and they produce their own building materials with the help of water. Water is needed to transport and dissolve a number of nutrients and also to maintain normal cell tension. The plant evaporates water and therefore makes sure that it does not "overheat". Even the most fertile soil cannot be productive without the addition of water.

However it is also not good to have too much water in the soil, since the water will displace the soil air. Plant roots need oxygen for their vital functions, so the roots never stretch deeper than the water table. When the groundwater level rises unexpectedly, or when water stays

Water is essential, among other things, to maintain cell tension. The water level must be topped up after evaporation!

These compost or manure worms live on manure and decayed vegetation (especially in the compost box).

on the ground for a long time, the plant roots die and so do the parts of the plant which are above ground, because they cannot get enough oxygen.

A water tap very close to your kitchen garden is almost a "must".

It is of course clear to everyone that plants need a constant supply of water. But what about the water supply in the soil?

The different water zones

If the groundwater level is not too high, there are three distinct water zones, from top to bottom.

The first zone which we can identify is the groundwater zone. No plant roots grow in this zone because all the pores are filled with water. The second zone which we encounter is the capillary layer. The water rises through the soil pores in this second zone. The level to which the water can rise depends on the size of the soil pores in these two zones. This process is called the capillary action of the soil.

Finally, the highest layer contains suspended water. This layer is not directly linked to the groundwater. After a heavy shower, a large proportion of the water sinks to the bottom, but a small amount remains suspended in the upper layer of the ground. Actually, this suspended water zone is similar to a sponge. If you immerse a sponge in a bowl of water and take it out without squeezing, a large quantity

TIP

To prevent radiation (evaporation) from dry soil it is wise to dig the soil very lightly just before a period of drought. This will break the capillaries and the available moisture will be retained better and used to the full.

of water will be released. The liquid that is still in the sponge is not heavy enough to fall out of it and remains suspended in the sponge.

Particularly on lighter soils (with large particles and large pores), the plants depend on the suspended water for their water supply. A soil type holds water well if there is a lot of water left behind in the suspended water zone after a shower. A constant supply of organic material will ensure that the soil can hold more water.

Watering

You should remember that if you water plants it does not make much sense simply to spray them a little. The water must reach the very finest roots of the plant. If you water plants every day, they absolutely will not be stimulated to make longer roots to search for deeper water. Not even the deepest-rooted plants can get at that little bit of water that you have sprayed on the surface.

A misting installation – with movable pipes – distributes the water so finely that the plants can get the maximum benefit from the moisture.

You will probably soon get fed up with spraying and watering by hand.
Use an oscillating or rotary sprayer or lay perforated hosepipes between the plants, then you can do something else in the meantime.

TIP

If there is a layer of clay under a sandy surface, water may rise in the narrow capillaries of the clay, but it will reach no further than the beginning of the sandy layer, where the capillaries are wider. Try to mix the soil layers so that the transition from clay to sand is more gradual. This will make it possible to retain the water better.

Working the soil

What is the best way of working the soil in your kitchen garden? Should you dig, rake, weed or, perhaps, mulch? You will find an answer to these questions in this chapter.

Digging the soil.

Every kitchen gardener naturally wants to get the maximum yield from the garden without exhausting the soil. They will need to dig, weed, rake and possibly even rotavate. In this chapter you will read about the various methods of working the soil which are needed if your plants are to attain maximum growth without ruining the structure of the soil or damaging the soil life.

Superficial digging

Superficial digging is mostly needed to work weeds, manure, compost and the like well through the soil and to break up heavy soil to give it more oxygen. You should, however, take care not to dig up any weed roots or fresh green material. Fresh material attracts soil insects such as wireworms and leatherjackets. Chop up all green compost and weeds before throwing them on the compost heap green. Do not dig weeds in and work manure and compost lightly into the top layer of the soil. If manure and compost are dug deeper into the ground, most of the nutrients which are released will leach out to layers further down and be lost.

Clay soil should preferably be dug before winter begins, and the soil should be allowed to lie rough. Since water expands when frozen, the large clods will crack open and break into smaller lumps and crumbs. Sandy soil has a naturally loose structure which is very fragile. It is, therefore wise not to dig sandy ground until the spring. Do not walk on ground which has not been dug. It is best to lay a few planks on the soil for manuring, composting or any other activities involving vehicles.

Deep digging

Deep digging (three spades deep) may be needed to loosen the subsoil so that the plant's roots can penetrate deep into the ground. Try to dig in such a way that the good topsoil stays on the surface: do not exchange the soil layers. A spade or shovel is the best tool to use in most cases, but we would recommend a digging fork for heavy clay soil, because the soil will not stick to it as much.

Other working methods

Digging – either surface or deep digging – is of course not the only way to work the soil of your kitchen garden. There are many other ways and we will describe the most common ones below. Choose the right method depending on the work you will be doing and your soil type.

When using a rotavator, the blades usually mix up the surface soil, which results in a crumbly surface. Particularly on heavier soils, where hand digging is very hard work, rotavators can be the solution. It is best not to rotavate if the soil is too wet, since it will cause the soil to be compacted. Unfortunately weed roots are cut into small pieces by the rotating small blades (they will produce more weeds as a result), and the various insects living in the top layer of soil also have a

TIP

After deep digging, first allow the soil to settle and only then work the manure or compost through the soil. You should not begin planting or sowing until two weeks later.

Use a garden fork to remove weed roots. This works better than a hoe, which can easily cut through the roots.

difficult time. We would not recommend rotavating sandy soil due to its fragile structure.

A **cultivator** is an ideal tool for working the topsoil. This garden tool can be used to work compost through the surface so that it stays light and airy.

A cultivator has teeth with a type of barb. Depending on the job, you can work the soil with 1, 3 or 5 teeth.

Use a **weeding-hook** and **hoe** to remove weeds and open up the surface after rain. The hoe should be pulled along, so that it turns over heavier soils only lightly.

Finally you should use the essential rake on clay soils. This is used to make the clods finer, press in the seed and make seed gullies. Do not buy a rake which is too wide. It is better if the rake is no wider than the distance between the rows in your kitchen garden. On sandy soil it is best to use a two, three or four-pronged fork or a fork with curved teeth where possible. A rake can break up the structure so much that the soil turns to dust.

A cultivator is an ideal tool for working the surface of the soil.

One item which should not be missing from your list of essential tools is the fork with curved prongs. You can use this to break up and spread manure. This fork is also an essential garden tool when it comes to putting green waste on the compost heap.

Pull out weeds between the onions by hand, then the soil structure will stay intact. The uprooted weeds can be left lying beside the row on dry, sunny days.

Removal of larger weeds is particularly likely to open up the soil between the carrots.

The weeds are laid between the rows. In dry weather they will shrivel up and you will not have to remove them. They also keep the ground between the plants covered.

Press down the soil between the carrots firmly after weeding, so as not to give the carrot fly a chance.

Mulching   All soil tends to become overgrown. Watch your kitchen garden carefully and see what happens after you have prepared the garden for the new season.

Within the shortest possible time there will be a veil of green covering it. Germinated seeds from outside are borne by the wind and animals, and they find a suitable place in your kitchen garden to germinate. Using cultivators, pulling up weeds and using the weeding-hook will again be necessary at this stage.

Weeds impoverish the ground because they take nutrients from the soil. But you should be careful when you remove the weeds, because sun, wind and rain will play havoc with the bare soil which is left behind. A lot of rain will cause important nutrients to be washed out of the soil, the sun will dry out the soil and greatly influences its temperature and finally the wind will blow away the soil particles (erosion) and also has a severe drying effect on the soil.

You can prevent all these problems by mulching and covering the soil at the right time. If you use organic material to cover it, this will combat weed growth and at the same time add nutrients.
There are even more reasons for mulching: it keeps the soil nice and damp, combats evaporation and erosion by wind and water and

TIP

Loosen the surface of the soil before you start to sow. Use a rake to break up the clumps finely and also mix some sand with the soil if necessary. To prevent structural damage, you should not work the soil at all when it is wet.

There is one disadvantage in using a net to protect your plants: it is less easy to keep them clean.

preserves the crumbly structure of the soil. You can use leaves, garden turf, cut grass, wood chips, tree bark, compost or sawdust from unpainted wood (no tropical hardwood) as a layer of mulch.

There are disadvantages if a layer of mulch is left in place all the year round. The organic material attracts snails, mice and moles. On wet soils the soil under the mulch layer will stay wet longer and will therefore be cold. Late night frosts cause more damage to plants in covered soil.

You can partly overcome these disadvantages by letting the uncovered soil come up to temperature early in the year, around mid-January, and then to begin mulching from mid-May. The layer of mulch should be no thicker than 5 cm. A layer which is too thick between the rows casts a shadow, so that young plants do not get enough light. Leave the mulch layer till about halfway through the following January.

Horizontal drainage

Improving drainage is also a way of working the soil. In the first chapter we dealt with vertical drainage: a way of breaking through impervious layers. On soil which is constantly wet, however, horizontal drainage may also help. In this case, dig trenches in the ground starting at the drainage ditch, just above the highest measured water

Currants love a layer of mulch: a thick layer of leaves has been used here.

Left: although you do not have to be so afraid of erosion with this soil, sun and wind will still have a drying effect. Rainfall makes the soil silt up. A covering in the form of a mulch layer is recommended.

level (summer and winter) using a drainage shovel. The distance between the trenches should be three metres, and they should have a slight slope inland. Line the bottom of the trenches with earthenware or plastic drainage pipes (corrugated pipes) and then fill the remainder with soil.

The soil will stay nice and loose under a layer of straw.

If you have made rather wider trenches using an ordinary shovel, you can spread a 20 cm thick layer of gravel or clay pellets on the bottom instead of using pipes. Lay a sheet of plastic on top and fill in the soil on top of that. If the drainage facility runs past trees or through an area planted with shrubs, it is best to use closed PVC pipes in those places, so that roots cannot penetrate them.

Of course horizontal drainage only makes sense if the pipes end in the drainage ditch above water level. You should also make sure that the pipes are buried deep enough not to cause problems when working the soil, and stay outside the root zone used by the plants.

Wood shavings can be used as a mulch layer. Do not forget to add some nitrogen if required.

TIP

Nitrogen is needed to convert a mulch layer which contains a lot of carbon (sawdust, straw and wood). If you do not mix any nitrogen with the mulch layer, it will be extracted from the soil. It is therefore best to add nitrogen when applying the mulch.

Right: you can raise up ground water using this hand pump.

Fertilising the ground

Healthy soil forms the basis for healthy plants. The first area to pay attention to when fertilising must once again be the soil.

Papilionaceous plants form nitrogen nodules on their roots as they grow.

The quality of the soil must be maintained and if necessary improved, especially with respect to its structure, pH value, ability to hold on to nutrients and the activity of soil organisms. Plants are better able to take up nutrients from soil which is bursting with life and has sufficient oxygen.

If you want to benefit from the stored nitrogen later, it is important not to uproot the entire papilionaceous plant after harvesting but to leave the roots in the soil.

The need to fertilise

Fertilising is not only necessary to improve the condition of the ground, but also to remedy shortages of nutrients in the ground and to keep the supply of humus at the right level. Many nutrients occur naturally in the soil. These substances are partly dissolved in the soil moisture and partly attached (adsorbed) to clay and humus particles in the soil.

This food is directly available to plants. A proportion of nutrients are stored in solid organic and inorganic compounds. Through erosion (of the stone which forms the soil: see chapter 1) and mineralisation, these nutrients become available to the plant very slowly. As nutrients are taken up, and also as they are blown away or leached out, shortages can arise. You can make up these deficiencies by fertilising the soil with organic fertilisers and through green manuring (particularly using papilionaceous flowers).

You can also replenish nutrient shortages by applying artificial fertilisers where necessary. In the latter case, however, no humus is formed.

The effect of the most common nutrients

Tests have shown that the following minerals are absolutely essential to plant growth: nitrogen, phosphorus, potassium, magnesium, calcium and a few trace elements.

Nitrogen

Nitrogen is marked with the letter N on fertiliser packaging. Nitrogen particularly influences the formation of proteins and chlorophyll in the plant. It is essential for the green, growing parts.

Papilionaceous plants, such as legumes, form tubercles on their roots with the help of soil bacteria. Nitrogen taken from the air by these soil bacteria is stored in these root tubercles, which is why they are called nitrogen tubercles. You can make use of this nitrogen by growing these papilionaceous plants in the same place as green vegetables.

After harvesting broad beans from the legume patch, young green vegetables can use the nitrogen which is released.

Nitrogen deficiency can be recognised by yellowing leaves and stunted growth. On the other hand a plant with too much nitrogen will be coloured blue-green and will be limp and highly susceptible to fungal diseases.

Nitrogen can be applied in the form of fast-working urea and nitrate, or in the form of slow working proteins and ammonia. Organic gardeners prefer the latter two types of nitrogen because they have to be converted by micro-organisms into nitrogen (nitrate) which can be

The purple colouring and stunted growth of these cauliflower leaves indicates dryness and nitrogen deficiency.

used by the plant. Although urea is an organic nitrogen compound, it can also be seen as an artificial fertiliser because of the way it works.

Phosphorus

Phosphorus is indicated on packets by the letter P, and it is important for the development of the roots, for flowers and for ripening of fruits and seeds. Phosphorus also affects the shelf-life of the product. Phosphate deficiency can be seen from delayed plant growth and poor development of lateral roots. If there is a phosphorus deficiency, the leaves will be a dark greenish-purple colour.

Potassium

The letter K on fertiliser packaging refers to potassium. This affects the formation of carbohydrates, which are found for example in the tubers of tuberous plants. Potassium also regulates the plant's water management system and improves resistance to disease. Above all, potassium improves the flavour and shelf-life of the product. A plant with withered leaf margins all too often indicates a shortage of potassium.

Magnesium

Magnesium, abbreviated to Mg, is necessary for chlorophyll formation. It also plays a part in transporting the various nutrients within the plant.
Magnesium deficiency can be seen by leaf discoloration: the leaf will be yellow, while the veins remain green.

Calcium

Calcium is only needed as a plant nutrient in very small quantities. Nevertheless this substance is vital for plants because calcium binds acids which would otherwise poison the body of the plant, such as oxalic acid. Calcium binds acids in the soil, it is necessary for the formation of humus, it improves the soil structure, affects the takeup of nutrients and promotes nitrogen fixing by bacteria.

Soil types which have little or no calcium are referred to as acid soils. The soil loses calcium when plants take it up, through leaching and through the use of acidic fertilisers. The calcium content in the soil is expressed as a pH-value (the hydrogen ion strength), which is also called its acidity.
Excessive calcium can mean that some nutrients become difficult for the plants to take up, while other nutrients are released and leached away.

Every soil has its own ideal calcium level. A clay soil should have a pH of about 7, while sandy soil should be between 5 and 6, sulphurous soil has an ideal pH of around 6.5 and peaty soil between 5 and 5.5. A pH level of 7 is called neutral; higher than 7 is calcium-rich (or basic) and lower than 7 is acidic. The more humus and clay particles the soil contains, the less the pH value will fall, even after the application of acidic fertilisers.

TIP

Look out for nitrite formation! Nitrite formation is promoted by the application of fast-working nitrogen fertilisers in the form of nitrate, by using excessively fresh manure, shortage of air in the soil and shortage of light during growth.

Magnesium deficiency first causes the edges of this endive's leaves to become a yellow colour. The veins stay green longest.

You can combat the acidification of the soil by applying calcium fertilisers, by adding extra clay granules and by working organic material into the soil. Organic material can also increase acidity or lower the pH. An average of 3 kg of chalk for every 100 square metres of soil is sufficient.

Trace elements

Since the beginning of this century, it has become clear that extremely small amounts of certain other elements are also needed to allow plants to grow at their best. Little is yet known about the exact function of these elements. It has, however, been found that a surplus or a shortage can both be harmful. A shortage of iron, for example, inhibits the proper development of chlorophyll and celeriac tubers exhibit a brown discoloration when suffering from boron deficiency. An overdose of copper (as found in pig manure) is not beneficial to your plants either. Sandy soils are particularly sensitive to this.

Fertilising with trace elements only makes sense if a genuine deficiency has been ascertained. Never forget that too much will always be harmful!

Organic fertiliser

If you want to fertilise not only the plant but also the soil, then you must use organic fertilisers. We make a distinction between unconcentrated organic fertilisers – such as real cow manure and compost –

> **TIP**
>
> **Spread chalk on dry ground preferably in the autumn or early spring and mix it well with the soil. Never apply chalk at the same time as organic manure or nitrogen and phosphate fertiliser. Leave a period of six weeks in between.**

Left: incompletely digested horse manure can be recognised by the obvious round shape of the horse dung.

Undigested straw-rich cow manure.

Here coral algae chalk which is rich in lime, magnesium and trace elements, is being scattered over the soil which is to be cultivated. Since coral algae chalk can also be taken up through the leaf, it can also be applied as a leaf fertiliser.

and concentrated organic fertilisers (including waste from abattoirs). You can use large quantities of unconcentrated organic (animal) fertilisers because their nutrient content is relatively low. These types of fertiliser contain the most organic matter of all, and they contain far lower quantities of trace elements.

If we look at the percentages of various nutrients in farmyard manure, we can see that the animal from which the dung comes has an important part to play here. Overall, cow and horse dung is preferable. All types of animal manure must be at least six months old. It should not be added to the soil too long before the new growing season. In order to prevent leaching by rain, you should dig in the manure as quickly as possible, just below the surface of the soil.

Apply a basic quantity of 500-600 litres of farmyard manure to every 100 square metres of soil.

Concentrated organic fertiliser

If you cannot get farmyard manure, this is not a disaster. You can still fertilise organically by using concentrated organic fertilisers. These fertilisers contain high concentrations of nutrients and also trace elements and a lot of organic material. Since you should consider some types of concentrated fertiliser as fresh manure, it is best to mix it into the topsoil at least two weeks before sowing and planting. A

TIP
Never spread chalk just for the sake of it, for example because it is likely to help if there is acid rain. Always test the pH level of your soil first. There are various testing kits, for example Rapitest, available in the shops.

To test the pH level of the soil, dig up a sample of soil with a trowel to a depth of about 5-15 cm.

Take a piece of soil from the soil layer using a knife or small spoon (not with your fingers).

Partially fill the rapitest test tube with soil (do not use your fingers).

The tube should be filled with soil up to 10 mm for this test. Read the instructions for other tests.

Add distilled water to a height of 35 mm (height in the tube).

Shake the tube for a minute until the tablet is dissolved.

Add a chalk tablet and put the bung in the tube.

Put the tube away and let the soil settle.

The solution will clear after 2-3 minutes and the colour can be compared with the colour table which is provided. In this case, the soil is very acidic.

This soil is much less acidic. On the basis of this test you can determine how much chalk you should add to the soil.

few well-known simple organic fertilisers are Faforiet, Culterra, Viano, Dendrovorm, Ecosol and Aglukon natural fertiliser. Widely used organic fertilisers are blood meal (13% nitrogen and 85% organic material), guano (bird dung containing 14% nitrogen) and horn meal, which contains 10% nitrogen and 5% phosphorus. The best one to use as a phosphate fertiliser is bone meal. The proportion of phosphoric acid is at least 18% and bone meal also contains 6% nitrogen and 30% calcium.

One disadvantage of powdered fertiliser is that you are dependent on the weather – powder will blow away in no time on windy days.

In addition to these concentrated fertilisers, other aids to organic gardening can be used such as coral algae chalk, basalt meal and bentonite clay. All concentrated fertilisers are available in the shops in both powdered and pellet form.

You can use 15 kg of concentrated mixed organic fertiliser for every 100 square metres as a basic fertiliser. Depending on what plant you are growing you can also use a simple organic fertiliser when growing begins.

Some organic gardeners use artificial fertilisers such as potash, basic slag, and sodium nitrate. The latter is originally a natural product. It works fast and is used in the case of a sudden nitrogen deficiency.

Granulated fertiliser is much easier to use.

Green manures   Sowing plants which are not intended for harvesting is known as green manuring.

31

Green manuring particularly influences the structure of the soil, since a covering of green manure prevents the soil from forming a crust. The use of green manure also supplies organic material and makes the soil more permeable thanks to the deep roots of plants such as lucerne and English rye grass. Finally, green manure prevents erosion and fix the nutrients. Papilionaceous plants used as green manure also keep up the level of nitrogen. Green manure is usually sown as a second crop in the winter which either freezes in the winter and is raked off or is dug in as late as possible. However, in order to prevent fresh material ending up in the soil (it attracts wireworms and leather-jackets), it is best to mow the green manure and return it to the garden via the compost heap. Green manure, like mulching, encourages snails and mice.

Do you recognise the flowers of this rape – a type of green manure?

T I P

Never use cruciferous flowers as green manure on soil which is infected with club root because these plants are highly susceptible to this disease. You must also take this into account when producing a growing plan for crop rotation.

Schedule for green manuring

Plant	Soil	Sowing time	Hardy	Comments
Alexandrian clover	clay	July-10 Aug.	very	produces nitrogen
Cabbage	all	July-20 Aug.	moderate	crucifer
False nettle	all	August	very	good cover, crucifer
Borage	all	March-September	very	good cover, attracts bees

Plant	Soil	Sowing time	Hardy	Comments
English rye grass	all	March-April	not very	deep rooted
Yellow mustard	all	August	very	cruciform
Barley	all	September	not	cover
Marigold	all	March-September	moderately	
Hop clover	all	March-April	moderately	produces nitrogen
Italian rye grass	all	April-May, July-20 Aug.	moderately	cover
Rape	all	August	reasonably	crucifer
Lucerne	all	March-June	reasonably	produces nitrogen
Lupin	sand	March-April	very	produces nitrogen
Phacelia	all	July-September	very	good cover, produces nitrogen
Red clover	all	March-May	not	produces nitrogen, cover
Birdsfoot	sand	July-15 Aug.	very	produces nitrogen
Spurrey	sand	August	very	large spurrey, gives fewer wild shoots
Turnip	all	July-Aug.	moderately	good cover, crucifer
Common vetch	clay	July-15 Aug	very	produces nitrogen
Winter rye	sand	September	not	makes the ground loose
White clover	all	March-May	moderately	produces nitrogen
Summer rye	sand	15 Aug.-15 Sept.	very	good cover

Rye grass has hardly any flowers, but it covers the ground extremely well.

Comments: plants which produce nitrogen are less appropriate as a preparatory crop for chicory, turnips and Brussels sprouts.

Artificial fertilisers

Artificial fertilisers only serve to fertilise the plant, and make no contribution to the soil. Fast-working artificial fertilisers give the plant a growth spurt during which it grows too fast for its own strength and increases the chance of pests. The advantage of fast-working artificial fertilisers is that they can be used to correct a deficiency quickly. Above all, artificial fertilisers are easy to apply and you always know that the percentage and exact ratio of the various nutrients has been precisely calculated.

Over-fertilising is harmful because plants can be scorched due to an excessively high concentration of salts. The risk of over-fertilising is obviously greater with artificial fertiliser than when you use organic fertiliser. Too much artificial fertiliser will leach out and pollute the environment. Apart from that, the production of artificial fertiliser also has a serious effect on the environment.

For a basic treatment you can use around 8 kg of compound (mixed) artificial fertiliser per 100 square metres.

TIP

Sow clover among your cabbage plants. Scientists have discovered that cabbage white butter-flies on the lookout for cabbages look for the specific shape of the vegetable. When there is clover underneath the cabbage, the cabbage does not show up against the soil beneath and it is therefore unrecognisable to the butterfly. Clover can also be used with other plants.

Choose fertiliser   The worse the soil structure (too wet, too sticky, too dry), the more important it is to use non-concentrated organic manure. This is because it contains the highest proportion of organic material. These nutrient materials are most effective in combination with green manure. If the soil does have a good structure, however, you can also use concentrated compound organic fertilisers on their own.

The best type of fertiliser to use depends on what nutrients are already in the soil. But since these nutrients are not visible to the naked eye you will have to carry out a soil investigation to determine exactly what nutrients your soil needs.

Be extremely careful about applying nutrients at random. This is because the takeup of specific nutrients by plants depends not only on their presence in the ground, but also on the presence of other nutrients. A shortage or surplus of a particular nutrient can prevent the takeup of other substances.

Right: however and whenever you sow lupins, do not let them go to seed, otherwise you will never get rid of this nitrogen-producing plant!

Marigolds are a very rewarding green manure which you can sow almost throughout the growing season.

Making compost

By making compost yourself you can kill two birds with one stone. You can save money while also producing a good soil improver which contains no heavy metals. Home-made compost is an organic product, improves the soil structure and also contains nutrients and trace elements.

A mixture of straw-rich and green waste.

Heap or box? Compost heaps can look very tidy, so you don't have to search for a hidden corner where they will not show. A sheltered area of garden which is partly shaded is the ideal site for a composting site. If you do not have much space, then you can use a barrel, although the conversion of material in a barrel does not always go smoothly. Decomposition is much more successful in a square box made of wire mesh or unpainted wood. A box of this kind also looks neat and tidy and you can make it as large as you like. Reserve a similar sized space next to the compost heap or box: then the first heap can be maturing while the second one is being built.

Setting up a compost heap Dig an area of soil about 1.5 - 2 m wide, and of whatever length you require, down to a depth of 10 cm. Loosen the subsoil and fill the shallow hole with a layer of thick stalks. This will allow surplus water to drain away easily. Do not use rough pruning wood, because you will be finding it in the compost for ever and a day. Apply a 2 cm layer of earth over the stalks.
Next comes a 20-30 cm thick layer of garden and kitchen waste, cut to hand size. This waste must be of animal or plant origin. Coarse and fine material should be alternated regularly. The nutritional value of the final compost will be substantially improved if you add manure (from chickens, pigeons, rabbits, goats etc.) to the compost heap from time to time.

COMPOST BOX

Comprises:

6 loose-laid pieces, with two

planks removable for scooping

out compost.

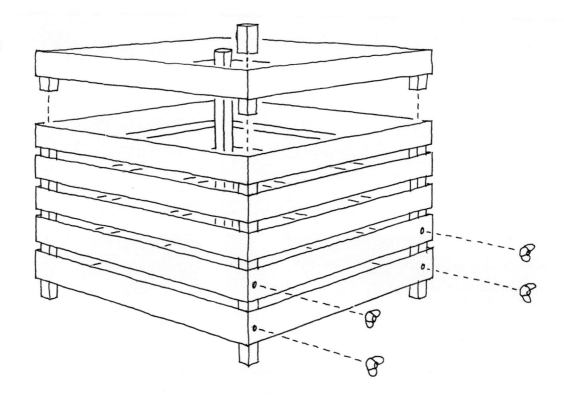

COMPOST HEAP

- covering layer: soil, leaves, grass,

  jute sacks, carpet or plant growth

  (e.g. pumpkins)

- garden and kitchen waste

- 1 cm soil

- thin layer of chalk

- garden and kitchen waste

- coarse material: wood chips,

  sunflower stems

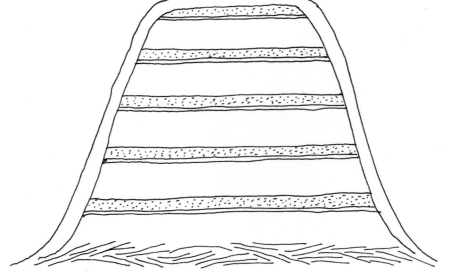

1 The coarse compost is shovelled onto a sieve.

2 The coarse compost particles are separated from the finer ones, depending on the width of the gauze mesh.

3 The coarse remains can be worked into a second compost heap. Bacteria and fungi can thus be introduced into the new heap.

4 The fine matter is collected under the sieve.

5 The sifted compost easily dries out unless you cover it. Work it into the seed gullies immediately after sifting, or cover it with a protective layer.

Next spread a wafer-thin layer of chalk on top of these layers of waste (as if you were sprinking icing sugar on a Yule log) and then another thin layer of soil or compost. The layer of chalk is necessary for smooth conversion. The earthworms which are largely responsible for the process, need the chalk for their work. We are not only talking about the common earthworm, but also the manure or compost worm which cannot survive in ordinary soil. Now start again from the beginning: first a new layer of waste, then some more chalk and another layer of soil. Build up the heap like this until it has reached a height of roughly 1.5 m. Finish off the compost heap by covering it with a layer of grass, an old carpet or some rush matting.

At this stage the heap can also be planted with nasturtiums, courgettes or pumpkins. This will prevent it from drying out. Leave it alone for at least six weeks and start a new compost heap next to it.

After six weeks you can remove the covering from the first compost heap. The top and outside of the heap may not yet have decomposed, but that is no problem at this stage. Scoop the remaining parts onto the second heap and the rest is ready for use. Note: waste around the outsides of a barrel or box made of plastic or wood will be converted more quickly than in a loose compost heap because the outside walls of a box or barrel are less subject to cooling.

The ideal composting site is partly shaded.

If you want to use compost as a sowing medium, all coarse and undigested parts must be removed.

39

Conditions for good conversion

Carbon and nitrogen should be present in the waste which you use for the compost heap in specific proportions. That is to say: 20 parts carbon (C) to 1 part nitrogen (N). Divide leafy material and stems evenly. Animal manure contains a lot of nitrogen and woody plants or those with many stems contain a lot of carbon. If there is too much carbon not much will happen in the compost heap. If there is too much nitrogen this may cause rotting and give off ammonia.

The following summary shows the ratio of carbon to nitrogen in various animal and vegetable wastes (the ideal ratio is 20:1):

urine or liquid manure	0.8:1
blood	3:1
chicken manure	6.3:1
vegetable waste	7:1
grass	12:1
farmyard manure	14:1
oat straw	48:1
wheat straw	128:1
fresh sawdust	511:1
rotted sawdust	208:1
kitchen waste	16:1
alder/ash leaves	25:1

Do not cover the heap with plastic, even if it is in the sun. The chance of incomplete conversion, overheating and rotting is very high.

T I P

You can add other substances besides chalk to the compost heap to increase its nutritional value: bentonite, lava or basalt meal (binds minerals which are released, reduces the odour and adds trace elements) and concentrated fertilisers, such as blood and horn meal (for more nitrogen), bone meal (for more calcium and phosphate) and Nitrate Chalk by Gem or vinasse (for more lime).

The temperature in a compost heap can rise so high that it begins to steam.

There are several so-called compost starters for sale on the market. If you add this agent to your compost heap, this will help to create the correct proportion of carbon and nitrogen. These compost starters also act as a nutrient medium for bacteria.

Make sure that the compost heap always gets enough air. In principle there will be enough air in a heap no higher than 1.5 m and no wider than 2 m. The length of the compost heap has no effect on this and is therefore unlimited. The heap must certainly not be too dry, but it should not be too wet either. In the first case almost nothing will happen and in the second case it will begin to stink because of the shortage of oxygen. In this case you should set up the compost heap again, adding some dry matter such as peat dust or straw.

The micro-organisms do the work

The presence of micro-organisms is indispensable for the conversion of waste into humus or compost. Bacteria, fungi, springtails, nematodes, etc. all need an oxygen-rich environment. The conversion process produces heat, which can raise the temperature of the compost heap to 70° C. Weed seeds and pathogenic organisms are killed at this temperature but unfortunately some do survive. Fungi are not always killed either. To be on the safe side, therefore, you should not throw any diseased plant material on the compost heap. Throw some tubers (old flower bulbs, potatoes, chicory tubers) onto the heap every so often to encourage worms, which use them as a

TIP

You can build air channels in the heap by positioning a pole every 1.5 m (lengthways) and placing the waste around it. The channel serves to aerate and ventilate at the same time. If the post (for example a pvc tube) has holes in it, you can add water and other substances while the heap is being formed.

If the ratio of straw to vegetation is correct, all the plant waste will be digested. Too much straw-rich waste makes for bad digestion. Too much vegetation will stink.

breeding place. You can also incorporate old home-made compost into the new heap. This is a way of transferring all sorts of organisms from the old heap into the new one.

Cutting the waste to hand size accelerates decomposition. You can set up a heap using horse manure (this makes it hotter). You can also turn the heap completely inside out after a period of time, placing the lowest layer at the top and the topmost layer in the middle – encouraging the decomposition of the waste.

TIP

Cabbage stalks digest very slowly. It is therefore better not to put them on the heap. If the cabbage has been suffering from club root, you should not take any risks at all. Keep the cabbage well away from the compost heap, otherwise there is a risk that you will spread the fungus throughout the entire garden!

Forbidden on the compost heap!

Cooked food and diseased plants should not be put on the compost heap. Although some fungi in the compost heap form antibodies against pathogenic organisms, this is still risky. Kitchen waste sometimes contains harmful materials, such as the antisprout on potato peelings (which inhibits growth), the fungicidal substances used on oranges and the pesticides used on cut flowers.

Apart from these, you can use almost anything else that is "healthy", except thick layers of grass or tree leaves, because there is almost no air in between them. The layers become firmly caked together and are not converted. You need 500-750 litres of compost per 100 square metres if you are using it as a basic fertiliser. When starting to grow different crops it will be necessary to supplement this compost with simple organic fertilisers.

Position and arrangement of the kitchen garden

Now we will look at some questions relating to the plants themselves. Where should the kitchen garden be situated and how should it be arranged? Should the plants be sheltered while they grow and is it beneficial to combine herbs and green vegetables?

An ivy hedge will grow as high as you like. Support the hedge with wire mesh.

Sunny and easily accessible

If the land around the house has not yet been divided up, you should site your kitchen garden in the sunniest and most sheltered place. Most green vegetables need about 6-8 hours of sunshine per day. It is also important for the kitchen garden to be situated close to the house and easily accessible. The fun soon disappears if you can only get to your coveted carrots by crossing lawns, borders and meadows on a rainy day. Always try to use the best-drained part of the plot as your kitchen garden and you already know that you can improve the fertility of the soil with the aid of fertiliser.

A hedge as protection

Most plants hate wind. Apart from the injuries and diseases which it causes, wind makes leaves stiffer and harder. Protection from northerly and westerly winds is therefore vital for vegetables, since most winds come from these directions. But don't forget what the east wind can do! This wind is particularly strong and dry in the spring and can seriously damage your plants. If you can, you should maintain a southerly aspect, keeping an eye on shade. You will also increase the likelihood of frost damage if you shelter your kitchen garden on all sides.

Anyone worth his or her salt will want to get as much out of the kitchen garden as they can. Sacrificing part of the kitchen garden for a hedge (as protection) is not usually a very popular idea. A hedge seems

A well-planned kitchen garden, which was sketched out before the season began.

43

to provide nothing but extra work and mess, and above all it takes up space which could have been used for a few rows of nice runner beans. You should consider using a protective hedge, since – as you will discover below – even a narrow hedge offers more benefits than ten extra bags of beans in the freezer.

The advantages of a hedge

Perhaps your kitchen garden used to be on a country road where only a tractor passed every now and again, but now there is a good chance that fast cars will be spewing out exhaust fumes all over your vegetables. Not a nice thought. In this case, a hedge can serve as a green buffer, for example the snowberry (Symphoricarpus albus) filters and purifies the air.

In exposed areas the wind gets everywhere. The nutrient-rich crumbs of topsoil only need a gust of wind and they will be blown away (erosion). Once again, a hedge can provide some protection. The best place to plant a windbreak hedge of this kind is on the north and west of the plot, and possibly on the east as well.

Planting hedges keeps the ground inside the kitchen garden warmer. In an open garden protected by hedges the warmer air higher up and the cold air lower down will mingle, but just above the ground it will stay warm. This is especially useful in the spring, since then the young

The sunniest and most sheltered place in this garden is reserved for the green vegetables.

Not an ideal location for the kitchen garden. Downdraughts and eddies can wreak havoc behind high, solid walls. Above all, most vegetables need more sunshine.

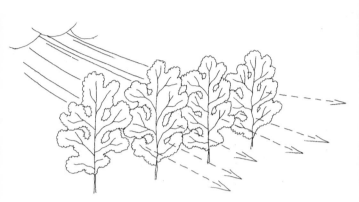

A hedge breaks (sifts) the wind.

plants can do without cold air. A garden which is walled on all sides has the reverse effect because it inhibits the mixing of the different air layers, so that the cold air is trapped and sinks to the ground.

An alder hedge cannot be kept very narrow, but it is very dense and full.

By reducing the strength of the wind, excessive evaporation is also prevented. Less wind means that the water vapour in the air above the plants will be removed less quickly. This is particularly important in the case of a sea wind, since the high salt content of the air means that it dries out the plants even more quickly.

Finally, a hedge encourages animal life in the kitchen garden. A hedge gives birds the chance to nest and birds consume harmful insects. Other useful insects such as predatory mites, ladybirds and ichneumon wasps find shelter there. Growing a hedge in your garden therefore allows you to create a special microclimate.

The disadvantages of a hedge

There are of course disadvantages associated with hedges. For one thing they will take up soil and they need nutrients and water for themselves. You can stop the roots of the garden hedge from searching for nutrients in the garden by chopping them off on the garden side each year and digging a trench and filling it with manure, so that the roots do not have to look for food further afield. In the first instance, it may seem that the hedge takes water from the crops, but once it has taken

TIP

Why not plant a hedge of bushes which have edible fruit? This will be not only attractive but tasty as well. Possibilities for an edible-fruit hedge include elder, blackthorn, apple rose, Japanese quince and blackberry. You can make juice, jam and jelly from all these fruits.

root and is growing, its roots will draw up water and nutrients from deeper layers in the soil.

Hedges cast a lot of shade. It is therefore best, certainly in small gardens, only to plant a hedge on the north and west sides.

It is a gross exaggeration to say that hedges are a source of disease. There are indeed a few diseases which can survive the winter in certain shrubs: black bean louse can winter on the spindletree, wheat rust on rhus integrifolia and bacterial blight feels at home on hawthorn and dwarf medlar, among others. You will see that many of these disadvantages can easily be overcome, so the on balance the advantages are more important, such as the usefulness of the hedge as a windbreak. The following shrubs and bushes can be considered for narrow, smooth-trimmed hedges: hawthorn, privet, hornbeam, beech, cedar, maple and yew. Hawthorn and privet are particularly good at coping with a sea breeze.

If your garden is so small that you really cannot spare a strip of ground for a hedge, then you should use fencing, for example made of rush matting, round wooden poles, windbreak netting, a fence made of willow twigs, wooden laths, railway sleepers or stones.

Whatever type of fence you choose, make sure the sides are left slightly "open". Closed fences or walls can cause swirling gusts and downdraughts.

Privet is an old favourite. This shrub is cheap, keeps its leaves almost until winter and can be kept narrow at any height. What more could you want?

Division of space On average, we estimate that a kitchen garden should cover 50 square metres per person and another 25 square metres for potatoes. Even if the garden is not very large, you will still need paths to allow easy access to all areas. The plants should be accessible by the main path (at least 60 cm wide) and, in larger gardens, by side paths. Grow the plants in beds no more than 120 cm wide. This width will allow you to do many of the necessary jobs easily. On wet soils it is recommended to lay the paths at a lower level and add the soil which is dug up to the beds. The excess water will then drain off the beds easily.

Reserve the shaded part of the garden for strawberries, endives, beetroot, rhubarb, celery, Swiss chard and redcurrants, whitecurrants and blackcurrants. Plants which require more sunshine and warmth can be planted on a slope in a kitchen garden without glass. Plants can get more of the sun's warmth on a south-facing slope (certainly if there is extra protection on the northern side). Try growing tomatoes, cucumbers, courgettes or melons on a slope of this kind.
The golden rule for every kitchen gardener should be to make a plan on paper each year to keep track of the crop rotation system.

Crop plan and crop rotation Crop rotation means never growing the same crop on the same piece of ground two years running. If you grow the same crop in the same place in a subsequent year, it will take exactly the same nutrients from the

TIP

How about a hedge of redcurrants and black-currants, raspberries, sweet corn, rows of garden and marrowfat peas and runner beans? Unfortunately it will not attract birds and insect life, but it will be very productive.

A rush mat takes up hardly any space at all. The mat sifts the wind and looks just right in a kitchen garden.

Sheltered between the greenhouse and the hedge, these edible pumpkins are being trained up the wall. Excess moisture (water vapour) is easier to remove (less disease) and the fruit will stay dryer.

soil and the root acids will release new nutrients intended for other crops which cannot benefit from them.

Even if you give plenty of manure, putting the same crop in again will exhaust the soil. There will be a shortage of nutrients and the plant will fall sick and die. The roots will be affected and the yield will fall. This whole process is called soil exhaustion and can affect any plant.

When you are sowing in the spring you will probably still remember what was in the garden the previous year and where it was. But remembering what was there two or three years ago is a lot harder. A crop plan is a useful tool to help you solve this problem.

The crop plan

The crop plan is a map of the kitchen garden showing which plants are being grown this year. The plants are divided into four groups to take into account their fertiliser needs and sensitivity to insects and fungi. Firstly there are the leafy plants, such as spinach, lettuce and cabbage. The second group contains root and tuberous plants such as beetroot, carrots, salsify and onions. In the third group come the fruiting and leguminous plants. Finally, potatoes, although they are a tuberous plant, form a separate group.

If you are not going to grow any potatoes at all, then you can use the space to grow annual cut flowers and/or annual herbs.

The decorative open concrete blocks act as a wall that lets the wind through.

TIP
Growing "warm" plants on a slope is definitely worth trying. Remember that the bottom of the slope will be colder and damper than on the slope itself. Cold air is heavier than warm air, which is why the air is colder at the bottom of the slope.

48

Of course this area must also be incorporated in the crop rotation diagram. It should be obvious that fruit trees will stay where they are, while fruiting plants such as currant bushes, blackberries and raspberries can be moved only once every ten years. Perennial herbs can be grown in the same place for five years.

Here part of the cultivation plan for the ornamental vegetable garden has been created in practice.

If you follow a crop rotation diagram, a section which has leafy plants in the first year will be occupied by root plants in the second year. Potatoes will then follow in the third year and legumes in the fourth.

Four or eight plots? Although some vegetables do not belong to the same group, they do not always have the same nutrient requirements: hence leeks (which count as tuberous vegetables), and celeriac are gluttons, while carrots, onions and chicory are definitely light eaters.

Part of a very attractive cultivation plan for an area of the ornamental vegetable garden at Huis Bingerden.

The leafy vegetables cauliflower, red, white and savoy cabbage and spinach need a lot of food, while lettuce, endive, Brussels sprouts and curly kale can manage on much less.

If you consider that some diseases can persist in the soil for more than four years, for example club root in cabbages, it would be better still to divide the garden into eight plots rather than four, and to divide the various plants into leafy I and leafy II, tuberous I and tuberous II, etc.

49

Combination growing

Combination growing means that you grow different plants one after another (early crop, main crop and late crop) and alongside each other, often in rows. In this way you can encourage the variety of vegetable and animal life on and in the soil. Often this will result in an improvement in quality, smell and taste.

Good combinations mean that certain diseases occur much less frequently, and certain combinations also provide an increased yield.

There is nothing strange about the fact that plants are affected by the plants growing directly next to them. Tall plants take light from lower plants and the roots of the different plants grow through each other. Plants can even compete for water and nutrients. However, tall plants can also provide shelter for warmth-loving low plants – for example, broad beans can shelter courgettes. In conclusion, all plants give off certain root acids which release nutrients which their neighbouring vegetables can use.

There is a great deal still to be discovered about how plants affect each other. A few tried and tested combinations are given with the tips in this chapter.

Carrots, onions and beets – all root vegetables – all together. They make the same demands on the soil.

If you use combination planting, you must take care that the plants do not hinder each other. Since the ground is actually used more intensively, combination planting requires not only extra work, but also more fertiliser.

The mutual influence is most beneficial if you sow rows of different plants alternately where possible. If you combine plants, you must still follow your crop rotation system.

Not a very favourable combination, but carrots and beets do make the same demands on the soil. They belong in the tuberous part of the garden.

Good combinations:
- potatoes and horseradish – increased yield
- beets and onions – encourage each other's growth
- radishes and cress – prevent flea-beetles
- lettuce and chervil – good heads of lettuce without aphids
- leeks, carrots and salsify – prevents attacks by leek fly
- tomatoes and African marigolds – good against whitefly
- cabbage and clover – the clover makes the cabbage unrecognisable to cabbage predators
- strawberries and green vegetables (particularly lettuce)

Bad combinations:
- dwarf beans and fennel – hinder each other's growth and flowering
- cabbage after radish and vice-versa – they attract the same insects

51

- lettuce and parsley – the lettuce gets a lot of aphids, and the parsley does not look nice either
- peas and beans – onions and shallots
- absolutely no cabbage plants between strawberries

Lettuce is also always named in the same breath as strawberries. An outstanding combination. Several leafy plants do extremely well between strawberries. Never combine strawberries with cabbages.

The cultivation plan – step by step

Bearing in mind the information which we have given you above, make a cultivation plan incorporating the following steps:

- measure the area of the garden and make a scale plan
- make a list of the plants you want
- sort the plants into groups: leaf, root, potatoes and fruit (possibly 2x leaf, 2x tuber, etc.)
- indicate by each plant how much space it needs
- look at a sowing/harvesting calendar to see whether two crops can follow each other
- divide the vegetables across the sectors (it will be clear if some have to be left out)
- fill any remaining spaces with herbs, flowers or green manure
- combinations of plants in the same group are ideal, for instance carrots and onions
- it is preferable not to cultivate vegetables in the same family during the same year (because of diseases): for example crucifers such as the various types of cabbage, radishes and cruciferous green manures;

- what is the fertiliser requirement of the various vegetables?
- what is the growing time required by a plant in connection with a subsequent crop?
- what combinations save space, such as lettuce (which does not have a large nutrient requirements) between runner beans?
- note which combinations of plants have a beneficial effect on each other

Glass and plastic in the vegetable garden

Flat cold frames, greenhouses and plastic structures (movable or otherwise) are often seen as part of the kitchen garden. It is always a pity to see that the cold frame is mostly only used as a "nurture area", while there are real opportunities to use it in other ways as well.

The flat frame

The standard flat cold frame is made of concrete or wood with a few intermediate laths, covered by single-window frames 80-150 cm wide. The high side of such a frame is usually 40 cm high, and the low side is 25 cm high. Some frames should be aligned east-west, so that the low side lies to the south and the contents of the frame get as much light as possible. A double frame which is slightly higher at the centre, about 50 cm, is usually aligned north-south so that both sides can receive equal amounts of light.

The flat cold frame has a high and a low side. Place a single row of frames in an east-west direction so that the plants will get the most sunshine.

First of all plant material can be nurtured in a flat cold frame. You can also sow and harvest earlier than is possible in the open and you can even start a new crop later in the year. You can use the frame ripen plants which would not survive outside in the colder parts of the country. Finally the frame can also be used for storage and silage of winter vegetables.

Light, air and heat In a frame the plants benefit from the sun's rays which pass through the glass, while the heat which the sun supplies does not disperse so fast to the outside. There is one disadvantage with this. Since the plants are not exposed to different weather conditions, the likelihood of disease is greater. The vegetables also tend to be limp.

In order to get the best possible growth, airing, sprinkling and screening techniques should be used. Due to the intensive use of the frame, it is advisable to replace the top 10 cm of soil with good gardening soil or compost every year.

In dull weather the temperature in the cold frame should be lower than when the sun is shining. Little sun combined with a high tem-peratures results in fast-growing, limp plants. Opening the windows of the frame in these conditions (airing) will cause the temperature to fall.

This round courgette grows well in the frame, whose windows are left off throughout the summer. The chance of bruising the leaves and stalks is very low because you can't stand inside it.

The cold frame is often only used for pre-sowing vegetables.

The air humidity in the cold frame can be very high. If you do not do anything about this there is a good chance that diseases and rot will set in. Once again airing is the solution, because this reduces and removes the excess water vapour. If, after starting the young plants off under glass, you plant them out in the open, you must allow them to become gradually accustomed to the climate outside. Hardening off means gradually airing more and more until the windows are left wide open all night. It is best to air the frame on the leeward side.

The blackberry partly shades the greenhouse from the sun. (Huis Bingerden)

Watering

You should remember that conditions are always (too) damp in a cold frame. Plants in a flat cold frame need more water than plants outside because of the warmer surroundings. It is better to water the young plants regularly rather than giving them a good drenching occasionally. If you do the latter this will result in excessive fluctuations in temperature and humidity. Never water in full sunshine and remember that the growth of plants will be hampered if the frame is too dry.

Fill the watering cans immediately after watering and put them in the greenhouse. This allows the water to come up to air temperature so that the plants will not be "shocked" by the cold water.

Protection

If the temperature in the frame rises too high you can keep out the sun by using protective mats. During a long hot summer it may be best to spray the windows with something that creates shade (something that will not be rained off) or a suspension of chalk in water. If you want to protect the frame against the cold, then the solution is rush matting or old clothes.

The hot frame In a hot frame extra heat is obtained by using fresh horse manure. Two to three weeks before you begin sowing, remove the soil from the frame to a depth of 40-50cm. Next lay a 25 cm thick layer of fresh horse manure mixed with straw, leaves or grass on the bottom of the frame (tread it down well). Finally apply a 25 cm thick layer of good soil. Put the windows on the frame and air the space now and then. The harmful gases released by the horse manure will be dispersed in this way. After a week or two you can sow or plant out into the hot frame.

Plastic as an aid In recent years there has been a tremendous increase in the use of plastic. Here are a few practical applications for the amateur gardener:

A plastic greenhouse If you want a greenhouse, a plastic greenhouse made of impregnated wood and reinforced sheeting is one possibility. A greenhouse of this kind can be stormproof, light and about 60% cheaper than a glass greenhouse.

No foundations are needed and the temperature is more even because the sunlight is tempered by the greenish sheeting. The sheeting will last no longer than ten years. It is worth considering before making your purchase that after about 10 years you will be left with some chemical waste.

Left: the African marigold is seen as an ideal soil disinfectant and prevents attack by whitefly. (Huis Bingerden)

This melon definitely will not fall off its stalk. It has been hung up in a pair of tights which are secured to the top of the greenhouse with string.

Left: cucumbers are trained upwards along strings in the greenhouse. Do not water the leaves, but the base.

TIP

If the sun suddenly begins shining very brightly, you can spread a shovelful of soil on the glass. Buttermilk poured on the glass also works well.

57

Tunnel cloches are relatively quite cheap. You can make these from bicycle rims and transparent sheeting and transparent material, but spring steel and cable sheathing can also be used. They are easy to build and dismantle, even during the season, and can therefore be incorporated into your crop rotation system. They can easily bring the growing season forward by six weeks.

A tunnel made of electricity cables covered with thick, transparent sheeting protects strawberries against night frost. This also brings the harvest forward.

Porous materials

The great advantage of so-called growth foil and Agryl sheeting is that airing and watering is not necessary: this is because the material is porous and stretches with the plants as they grow. Growth sleeves for tomatoes retain too much moisture, although they are perforated. The high air humidity therefore causes more disease in tomatoes.

When covering the ground with perforated foil or Agryl sheeting, use a piece much larger than the growing area. This is because the plants underneath will usually grow upwards. Ensure that the material is fixed securely at the edges.

Left: a sheeting greenhouse does not need foundations. Keep the sheeting as clean as possible so that it lets enough light through.

The plants growing under the sheeting can be harvested 14 days earlier. These materials, particularly Agryl sheeting, are extremely vulnerable and will last for no more than two years.

Particularly when growing early and late green vegetables, use clean, clear sheeting so that the plants can get as much light as possible.

This is because if not enough light reaches the plants the nitrate content of the leafy vegetables will increase tremendously.

T I P

If you want to protect individual plants against snails or cultivate young plants in warm, protected conditions, an ordinary I litre (or better still a 2 litre) plastic bottle will do. Cut off the bottom and place the cylinder over the young plant.

Here perforated sheeting has been used to protect germinating seedlings in the open soil from wood pigeons and crows. The sheeting lets light and water through.

The windows of this greenhouse have been treated with BioCoolglass. This softens the bright sunlight.

The sheeting can be removed. The plant is big enough and will be left alone by the birds. The plant also needs more light in order to develop properly.

Below: When it rains, BioCoolglass seems to dissolve and disappear. The windows become temporarily transparent. As soon as the sun returns, the substance protects the windows again. In the autumn, during long periods of rain, it disappears completely.

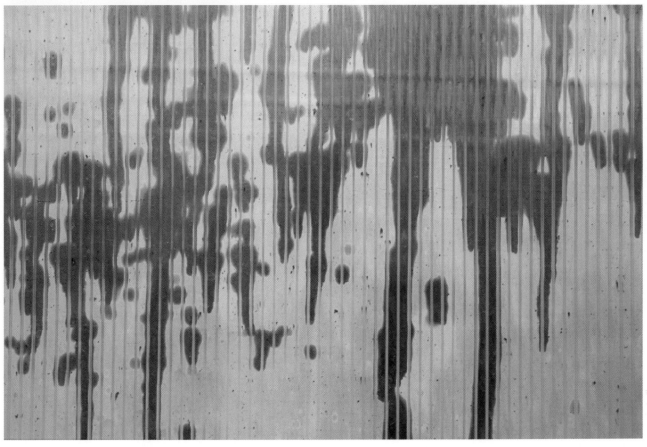

Vegetables:
Varieties and seeds

What could be better

than choosing vegetable

varieties and seeds.

Most people do this at a

time when there is not much to do in the

garden. Make your selection with the help

of the cultivation plan.

Different vegetables, different requirements

Unfortunately you cannot grow everything in your kitchen garden. Different vegetables have different requirements, so that leafy plants need water-retaining, nitrogen-rich soil, while iceberg lettuce and spinach need far more nutrients than endives and other lettuce varieties.

Many cabbage-type varieties make such high demands on soil nutrient levels that some gardeners allocate a separate plot to cabbages in the crop rotation plan.

Acid or chalk

The acidity of the soil also has a part to play. Hence plants like cabbage, spinach, beets and onions want a high pH level (a lot of chalk). This is in contrast to potatoes, for example, which thrive much better in an acid soil (low pH).

If you are gardening on lighter, nitrogen-rich soil which is not acidic, then it is better to grow green cauliflower, broccoli, savoy cabbage, curly kale, oxheart cabbage and Chinese cabbage rather than green, red or white cabbage or cauliflower, all of which prefer clay soil.

Vegetable and soil

It is now possible to make a specific choice of varieties. In the case of curly kale, for example, the Fribor F1 hybrid is only suitable for growing on heavier soil, while the Arpad F1 hybrid (Westland winter curly kale) is also suitable for lighter soils. In general it can be said that leafy plants will flourish in soil which has been well fertilised the

Brussels sprouts stay in the garden a long time and have to continue growing without stagnating. Give sufficient nutrients, but not too much nitrogen, otherwise there will be too many leaves. Brussels sprouts are very easy to grow on chalky soils and withstand frost well.

Above left: iceberg lettuce needs more nutrients than other lettuce varieties.

Lettuce does not need any extra fertiliser. Do not force lettuce and do not grow it in the "darker" seasons. The chance of nitrite being formed will be higher if you do!

same year. Root vegetables need good, loose-worked, fine-grained and water-retaining soil. They absolutely do not like farmyard manure which has been worked in the same year. On the contrary, they grow best on "old power", i.e. on a plot of land that was fertilised with farmyard manure during the last year. You can give them some compost first.

In thick, poorly worked soil roots begin to branch out. Some root and tuberous plants need extra feeding. Particularly celeriac, because of its long growing period, and leeks will be very thankful for extra fertiliser. You should fertilise celeriac with a fertiliser containing potassium, for example "vinassekali" (sugarbeet vinasse), and leeks need a nitrogenous fertiliser such as blood meal.

Following page: leeks like a lot of food, but not fresh manure, since it attracts flies. Plenty of compost and blood meal make a good fertiliser. Combinations of root vegetables and celery are said to fend off disease.

As for legumes, their nutritional requirements do not demand much from the soil. Half the amount of organic fertiliser (see chapter 3) will do for the basic treatment. Do not use fertiliser which contains a lot of nitrogen. The soil should be loosened to a good depth and should retain sufficient moisture.

Fruiting plants, which generally thrive well in warm conditions, are classified with the legumes in the 1:4 crop rotation scheme (with four groups). These do, however, need more nutrition. The normal basic fertiliser treatment will be sufficient, provided it does not contain too much nitrogen.

All root and tuberous plants, which includes shallots, grow best on a patch of soil which was fertilised with farmyard manure the previous year. Enrich your soil with some compost before you start cultivating.

The best location In order to prevent damage by insects such as root, leek and cabbage fly and gallfly, you should plant root plants, cabbages and leeks "in the wind". The above-named insects find it very difficult to land in windy conditions. Since fungi also grow well in warm, humid conditions, plants which are susceptible to fungal diseases, such as lettuce, should be planted further apart in less windy locations.

Broad beans and maize are good examples of wind-flowering plants. Among other things the wind ensures that the pollen is dispersed. Plant the rows some distance away from each other, otherwise the wind cannot get between them and poor fruiting will result.

Resistance You should also consider resistance to specific diseases when selecting varieties. Resistance means that a variety is not insensitive to a specific disease. Many varieties of beans are now resistant to the mosaic virus and fungal diseases.
In the case of other green vegetables you can select varieties from the catalogue which are not susceptible to withering, premature flowering or fungi.

Seed secrets Some vegetables need very little seed. Since different seed suppliers provide different amounts of seed, you may end up with a surplus.

Do not sow endives out until late June because the soil will only then be warm enough. If you sow endives in the cold the plants will probably overshoot later on.

TIP

So-called nitrogen nodules develop on legumes (see chapter 3). The following (leafy) vegtables cannot benefit from the rel eased nitrogen until after the legumes are harvested. You should therefore cut off the foliage and leave the roots in the soil.

This is not a bad thing, as long as you know how long the seed will remain viable. This list gives the viability period of various seeds:

1 year: salsify, sweetcorn, onions, leeks, parsnips and courgettes

2 years: beans and parsley

3 years: peas, carrots, purslane and chicory

4 years: beets, tomatoes, cabbage, spinach, marrowfat peas and lettuce

5 years: endive, cucumber, radish, Swiss chard, turnip tops and winter radish. Celery, melon and gherkin seeds can be kept even longer.

Do not forget, however, that you must keep all seeds cool and dry.

F1 hybrid

Sometimes, after a variety name, the term F1 hybrid is added, for example, Chiko F1 hybrid (Chinese cabbage). This means that you can expect a uniformly growing plant. In this case the Chinese cabbage will have long, well-closed, thick heads.

F1 (*filius* is Latin for son) is the first son of two inbreeding lines after cross-pollination. All the positive characteristics of several parents and grandparents are united in this "child".

Pre-soaking and pre-germination

Whenever you sow parsley, carrots, celery, beets, spinach and maize, you will notice that there is an endlessly long wait before the seed begins to germinate. In the meantime, you must keep the seed moist and chase off the birds. If you want germination to take place faster than usual, you can pre-soak or pre-germinate the seeds.

TIP

You can test the germinating power of a seed as follows: put a number of seeds in a small dish between two layers of blotting paper. Moisten the whole assembly and put it away in a damp, warm place. After one week more than half the seeds ought to have germinated, otherwise the seed is not worth using.

Maize needs the wind to set its fruit. Maintain a distance of 75 cm between the rows.

Pre-soaking means placing the seeds in tepid water for 24 hours; the water should be changed after 12 hours. Pre-germination means mixing the seed with damp sharp sand. The whole mixture should be put away in a damp, warm place until the seeds begin to germinate. Afterwards, the seeds must be planted out very carefully, sand and all.

Sowing The seeds can be sown directly in their intended location, but people very often do decide to pre-sow. As you read earlier, you can pre-sow outside in a cold (flat) frame, but you can also use seed trays indoors. If you want to ensure that the plants do not occupy the beds for too long, you can also pre-sow on seed beds outdoors.

After the seeds, which are often sown too close together, begin to come up, the plants are thinned or pricked out and may be put into forcing pots. They will then need more nurturing and hardening off, after which you can plant them outside in their intended location.

When sowing on location, a distinction is made between sowing in rows and broadcasting. Broadcasting is a technique not often used because of the need to keep the crops free of weeds. An exception is sometimes made for purslane, spinach and carrots. When sowing in rows, the distance between and within the rows depends on the plant. You will find information about this on the back of the seed packet.

TIP

FI hybrid seed is often expensive. Resist the temptation to self-seed from an FI hybrid. The next generation will have a very variable appearance and also variable quality. Negative characteristics will emerge again.

Above left: first loosen the soil in the rows and the moisten before sowing.
Above right: carrot seed is mixed with celery seed to test whether this combination has a favourable effect.
Below left: sow the seed as thinly as possible in the gully.
Below right: rake the soil carefully over the seed.

Right: You can grow round carrots even on very heavy soils.

How deep? If the distances are known, mark small gullies along a planting line. The depth of the gully depends on the size of the seed and the soil type; on sandy soil the gullies have to be twice as deep as on clay soil. On clay soil fine carrot and lettuce seed should be sown in gullies 0.25cm deep. Small seeds like cabbage and radish are sown 0.5cm deep. Medium-sized beet and spinach seeds need a 1cm gully, while 1.5cm should be enough for larger seeds such as French beans and peas. Finally, you must bury the very large seeds such as maize and broad beans at a depth of 2cm. One exception is onion seed, which should also be sown at a depth of 2cm. Moisten the seed gully before sowing and after sowing carefully smooth the soil over the seed and press down lightly. After the seed has come up, thin out the seedlings as soon as possible. Beans and other large seeds are often sown directly in their final position, but you should once again thin out the seedlings after they come up to leave the strongest plants.

"Special" growing tips In order to make sure that you will be able to harvest and eat all those tasty vegetables and all that luscious fruit, here are a few special tips to prevent disappointments, since after all the trouble you have put into your kitchen garden it takes all the fun out of it if you don't get a harvest.

Strawberries Strawberries prefer soil which is loosened quite deep down, contains humus and holds moisture well. Do not plant them too deep, how-

Left: you can use a lot of pruned wood as growing poles. Here runner beans are being trained up a frame of, among other things, beech twigs. You can use whatever wood you have available from pruning.

Self seeding is a painstaking business. The advantage is that the descendants will be better suited to your soil type, but the disadvantage is that racial purity will be lost and diseases such as viruses will be passed on to the next generation.

Plant leeks very deep and do not press down the soil around the plants.

ever, since that will hamper regrowth and budding and increase the likelihood of fungal problems. The planting technique is a very precise one. Make a reasonably large planting hole, build a small mound inside the hole and spread the strawberry roots over it carefully. Cover the roots with soil and press down well. Take care to ensure that the heart of the plant is level with the ground. Make sure there is an adequate water supply during the regrowth period.

Endives

Endives can be sown in the open around midsummer. The ground should be sufficiently warm if the crop is to succeed. If you sow in soil which is too cold, the endive will tend to grow uncontrollably later on. The same applies to chinese cabbage, sugar loaf chicory and radiccio. These should be sown in position and not transplanted, otherwise they will shoot out of control.

Beans

French beans have a relatively short growing period and you can harvest them slightly earlier than runner beans, which give a higher yield but suffer more from fungal diseases. French beans grown on sticks are the very weakest variety of bean and they are often a failure, particularly on damp, acid soils. You should try the much stronger scarlet runner: this plant will not cause many problems but must be harvested early.

Wet and cold are the arch-enemies of all beans. In wet years the beans

The endives which you want to harvest in June/July must be sown and grown in warm conditions (around 20°C). These endives can be planted outside after 1 May.

TIP

There are various aids such as pellet seed, seed tapes and seed rolls which are intended to make sowing easier but unfortunately most of them are quite expensive. On the other hand, a seed box, which can be adjusted for seeds of various sizes, is cheap and handy to use.

The male flower grows at the top of the maize plant.

sometimes do not germinate because the seeds rot away. In drier conditions the seeds can dry out. In order to be sure of germination in both cases, you should mix the seeds with salad oil or liquid green soap before sowing. This greasy layer ensures that the seed does not dry out and can survive in a very damp environment.

The female inflorescence grows from the leaf axil.

Cabbage and club root

Anyone who has ever grown cabbage will know (almost) all about club root. This disease is caused by a schizomycete (fission fungus), which attacks the roots of all cruciferous plants. A web of tissue grows among the roots, so that the roots become unable to take up sufficient water and nutrients from the ground. The plant withers and takes on a dull, lead-coloured tint. Knobby thickenings appear on the roots.

The fungus prefers acid, light soils and can remain in the ground for years. Maintain a crop rotation of at least 1:5 (five different groups) and try to lower the acidity by adding chalk. You can still try to cultivate infected soil in the spring because the fungus only becomes active above 16°C. If you want to grow cabbage but do not want to wait until the soil has improved, you can use large, bottomless pots filled with calcium-rich compost.

Bury the pots in the soil up to the rim.

TIP

All crucifers are susceptible to club root and radishes, winter radishes and turnip tops are all vegetables which belong to this family. But there are also crucifers used as green manures and ornamental plants. Take this into account in the crop rotation chart and let them "work together" in the cabbage patch.

Maize
Maize needs the wind for fruiting. You should therefore maintain a distance of 75 cm between the rows. Maize seeds are large enough to be pushed into the ground individually. Plant the seeds in rows, with a distance of 25 cm between seeds. A thick layer of compost between the rows prevents the roots from drying out and also provides extra nutrients.

You will usually harvest two or three cobs from each plant. A good indication of the right time to harvest is that the cob threads, known as "the beard", turn a darker colour. Ripe cobs can usually be easily broken off from the leaf axil by hand.

The cob is ripe when the cob tassel, the "beard", is completely dry and dark brown in colour.

Leeks
Since leek roots need a lot of oxygen and develop best in loose soil, and also because we like to see a long white shank, you must plant the leek plant very deep. Make a shallow furrow along a planting line and make deep holes (you can go down up to about 18 cm deep) using a planting stick. Then place the leek plants in these holes. We have consciously not said "plant" them, since that would suggest pressing down the soil.

Do the opposite: leave the plants standing loose in the holes with the heart open and bare. The roots will get enough oxygen. The holes will slowly fill up with soil by themselves, due to rainfall. Keep an eye on them in dry periods, when you should water the furrow so that the holes gradually silt up.

After pollination has taken place, the female inflorescence grows into a maize cob.

Some gardeners make a dilute mixture of cow manure for their leek plants and dip the leek roots into this. The plants stay upright much better and begin to grow immediately. Do not make the mixture too strong, otherwise the method has the opposite effect.

Radishes   Radishes absolutely insist on damp soil while they are growing. A constant water supply is therefore important, since the radishes need to grow continuously. If the water uptake of the root does not match the evaporation from the leaf, the radishes will be dry and sharp. It is not desirable to apply fertiliser, but a generous amount of compost is a good idea because a damp surface deters flea beetles. If you do not have any compost available, spread chalk or wood ash since flea beetles dislike these as well. Above all it is better for the soil to be on the chalky side.

To protect beans against wet and dry conditions during the germination period, mix them with salad oil or liquid green soap.

Lettuce   Calcium-rich compost is a good basic fertiliser for all varieties of lettuce. A study of the soil can show whether additional fertiliser is needed or not. You should remember, however, that over-fertilising is never good and you should be particularly careful if you apply a lot of nitrogen, since there is a risk that the nitrate level in the lettuce will be unnecessarily high.

Cabbage lettuce tends to overshoot for many reasons. First of all the wrong variety is often used for the wrong season. Find out which

Young radiccio. Radiccio forms a small head and is slightly bitter to taste. Sow radiccio in July.

varieties are suitable for early growing (for example, Meikönigin, and which are suitable for growing during the summer and autumn. The variety "Four seasons miracle" is an exception. This lettuce, which is soft as butter, with reddish-brown bobbled leaves, likes every season. Lettuce also has a tendency to overshoot if sown when the soil temperature is too high. Transplanted lettuce tends to overshoot more readily than lettuce sown on location.

Spinach

There are both sharp and round types of spinach seed on the market. It is recommended to use sharp-seeded varieties for winter growing. These germinate better in low temperatures and need less light than the rounded-seed varieties, which are meant to be sown outside in the late spring and summer.

Broad beans

Broad beans love a windy spot. The more the wind can blow between the rows, the better the fruiting will be. Plant broad beans in soil that has been loosened quite deep down at intervals of 10-15 cm and maintain a distance of 70 cm between rows.

If you have to shorten the long tap roots while replanting, this is not very serious. Plants with shortened roots may not grow as tall, but they will begin to flower earlier. For this reason gardeners sometimes cut the tap root through with a spade even if the broad beans are being transplanted.

An attractive alternative to spinach. New Zealand spinach – not in the spinach family, despite the name! You eat the tops and the leaves. Flowering and seeding do not affect the taste of the leaves.

Chicory   As long as they are in the soil, chicory roots are well able to withstand frost very well. But as soon as the roots have been dug up and are lying on the ground, they are extremely vulnerable. Those roots which you do not need for forcing inside can be left in the garden for a time. Usually chicory roots are dug up in October or November. After digging up the roots and allowing them to ripen in the field if applicable, the foliage is cut off a few centimetres above the root. The growth point should be visible.

Chicory in the summer. It looks just like a leafy plant.

Carrots   The greatest threat to carrots is the carrot fly, which likes to lay its eggs in loosely-worked, open soil. Since the first carrot flies might already be airborne in late April, you should make sure that you have done all your sowing by that time and the soil is closed and compact.

Try to sow carrot seeds so sparingly that the plants do not have to be thinned out any more, because every time you open up the soil (allowing air in), you will increase the chance of admitting small worms. Pull up the weeds between the rows early and avoid using the weeding-hook. When you finally begin harvesting, you should never pull out the thickest ones first. The tops of the carrots growing next to them will then be left uncovered and the carrot fly will lay its eggs there. After you have pulled out the carrots you need, tread the soil down firmly again.

Leave the chicory lying outside for a few days after digging it up.

Sowing calendar

Flowers

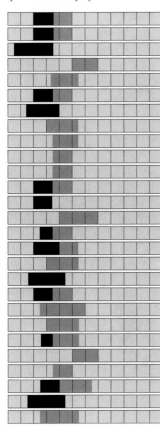

	J F M A M J J A S O N D
African marigold	
Ageratum	
Alyssum	
Carnations	
Aster	
Begonia	
Chrysanthemum	
Cineraria maritima	
Clarkia	
Cosmos	
Dahlia	
Dried flowers	
Sweet Williams	
Gazania	
Geranium	
Gypsophila	
Godetia	
Marigold	
Cockscomb	
Love in a mist	
House plants	
Climbing bindweed	
Cornflower	
Lathyrus	
Lavatera	
Snapdragon	
Lobelia	

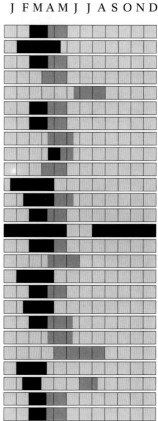

	J F M A M J J A S O N D
Lupin	
Daisy	
Wallflower	
Nemesia	
Nasturtium	
Poppy	
Petunia	
Phlox	
Portulaca	
Primula	
Larkspur	
Salvia	
Scabiosa	
Candytuft	
Ornamental gourd	
Slaapmutsje	
Tobacco plant	
Perennial plants	
Verbena	
Forget-me-not	
Violet	
Busy Lizzy	
Ice plant	
Zinnia	
Summer pansies	
Sunflowers	

■ Sow under glass
☐ Sow in rich soil
☐ Harvest

Left: salsify is an easy vegetable which can stay in the vegetable patch from April to October and can be harvested from the end of October onwards.

Vegetables

Sowing/planting periods chart (months: J F M A M J J A S O N D) shown as a colour-coded bar chart for each vegetable.

Vegetables	J F M A M J J A S O N D	1 packet is enough for:	Sow/planting distance between rows	within the row	deep freeze
Strawberries	(chart)	around 600 plants	45 cm	45 cm	
Endive	(chart)	around 500 plants	30 cm	30 cm	*
Artichokes	(chart)	around 100 plants	100 cm	80 cm	
Aubergine	(chart)	around 100 plants	45 cm	45 cm	
Gherkins	(chart)	around 15 m²	100 cm	15 cm	
Beet/beetroot	(chart)	around 10 m²	35 cm	10 cm	*
Brussels chicory	(chart)	around 10 m²	30 cm	10 cm	
Sugar loaf chicory	(chart)	around 10 m²	30 cm	10 cm	*
Chervil	(chart)	around 2 m²	25 cm		
Cucumbers	(chart)	around 10 m²	100 cm	15 cm	
Cauliflower	(chart)	around 200 plants	60 cm	60 cm	*
Broccoli	(chart)	around 250 plants	45 cm	45 cm	*
Curly kale	(chart)	around 300 plants	45 cm	45 cm	*
Chinese cabbage	(chart)	8 m²	30 cm	15 cm	*
Red cabbage	(chart)	around 200 plants	60 cm	60 cm	*
Savoy cabbage	(chart)	around 200 plants	60 cm	60 cm	*
White cabbage	(chart)	around 200 plants	60 cm	60 cm	*
Brussels sprouts	(chart)	around 200 plants	60 cm	60 cm	*
Kohlrabi	(chart)	around 200 plants	45 cm	45 cm	*
Swede	(chart)	10 m²	35 cm	25 cm	*
Sweetcorn	(chart)	3 m²	50 cm	30 cm	
Melons	(chart)	12 plants	1 plant per frame		
Peppers(paprika	(chart)	150 plants	50 cm	35 cm	*
Pepper	(chart)	around 200 plants	50 cm	35 cm	*
Parsley	(chart)	around 10 m²	30 cm		
Pumpkins	(chart)	around 15 plants	100 cm	15 cm	
Purslane	(chart)	around 2 m²	broadcast		
Leeks	(chart)	around 350 plants	30 cm	10 cm	*
Turnip tops	(chart)	around 5 m²	broadcast		
Radish	(chart)	around 3 m²	25 cm		
China grass	(chart)	around 3 m²	30 cm	10 cm	
Turnips	(chart)	around 5 m²	30 cm	10 cm	
Salsify	(chart)	around 2 m²	30 cm	15 cm	*
Celeriac	(chart)	around 300 plants	30 cm	30 cm	*
Blanched celery	(chart)	around 500 plants	30 cm	30 cm	*
Cutting celery	(chart)	around 4 m²	25 cm		
Common lettuce	(chart)	around 500 plants	30 cm	30 cm	
Lettuce	(chart)	around 500 plants	30 cm	30 cm	
Cabbage lettuce	(chart)	around 10 m²	30 cm		
Cos lettuce	(chart)	m²	30 cm		
Lamb's lettuce	(chart)	around 8 m²	30 cm		
Swiss chard	(chart)	around 5 m²	30 cm		
Spinach	(chart)	around 5 m²	25 cm		*
Tomatoes	(chart)	around 150 plants	45 cm	45 cm	
Garden cress	(chart)	around 3 m²	broadcast		
Onions	(chart)	around 5 m²	30 cm	10 cm	
Carrots	(chart)	around 12 m²	35 cm		*
Sorrel	(chart)	around 2 m²	25 cm		
Scarlet runner and runner beans	(chart)	around 12 m²	4 beans per pole		*
Dwarf beans	(chart)	around 10 m²	40 cm	10 cm	*
Broad beans	(chart)	around 5 m²	60 cm	15 cm	*
Garden peas and legumes	(chart)	around 7 m²	40/60 cm	7 cm	*

Vegetables

J F M A M J J A S O N D

- Strawberries
- Andijvie
- Artichokes
- Aubergines
- Gherkins
- Beet/beetroot
- Brussels chicory
- Sugar loaf chicory/radicio
- Chervil
- Cucumbers
- Cauliflower
- Broccoli
- Curly kale
- Chinese cabbage
- Red cabbage
- Savoy cabbage
- White cabbage
- Brussels sprouts
- Kohlrabi
- Swedes
- Sweetcorn
- Melons
- Peppers (paprika)
- Pepper
- Parsley
- Pumpkins
- Purslane
- Leeks
- Turnip tops
- Radish
- China grass
- Turnips
- Salsify
- Celeriac
- Blanched celery
- Celery
- Common lettuce
- Lettuce
- Cabbage lettuce
- Cos lettuce
- Lamb's lettuce
- Swiss chard
- Spinach
- Tomatoes
- Garden cress
- Onions
- autumn/winter/summer
- Carrots
- Zuring
- Scarlet runner and runner beans
- Broad beans
- Garden peas and legumes

Preventing and controlling pests and diseases

It is all very well if growing vegetables goes according to the textbook, but what should you do when that plague of aphids affects every single lettuce, and how should you deal with the worms in the strawberries?

Natural balance   One reason why amateur gardeners grow their own vegetables is because they want to grow their plants without using "poisonous" pesticides, so that they know what they are eating. In order to minimise the harm caused by pests and diseases, you should grow your plants under ideal conditions. You should try to achieve a natural balance in your kitchen garden. This is also a way to contribute towards a cleaner environment.

Snails are mad about large, tender leaves. A combination of mulch and moisture attracts them. Trap them with a sip of beer.

Here are a few methods which can contribute towards a natural equilibrium:
- work the soil as little as possible (to preserve soil bacteria)
- use organic, slow-working fertilisers
- choose plants suitable for your soil type
- choose the right site for your plants (carrots "in the wind", tomatoes and melons in a warm, sheltered place)
- use crop rotation and combination planting methods
- make use of resistant seed varieties
- take care to sow and plant at suitable distances to prevent fungi
- remove weeds regularly and never let them survive the winter (aphids winter on orache, chickweed and groundsel; club root fungus on shepherd's purse, Gallant Soldier and ivy)
- plant a hedge (a good nesting-place for birds) and sow and plant lots of herbs (to protect against insects and fungi)

Be on your guard against everything that flies.

- remove sick plants from the garden in good time and do not throw them on the compost heap

Another measure which you can take yourself. Put up nesting boxes, since birds consume pests.

Should a disease or epidemic raise its ugly head despite all these measures, try to control it by using a method which causes as little damage to the environment as possible.

If you consider that there are other animals and lower plants using a specific vegetable as a food source as well as you, this makes it clear that you, as a consumer, have competition. The odd thing is that when it comes to consumption, we do not take the other living organisms within our kitchen garden into account. Even environmentally friendly or organic gardeners are to some extent therefore acting contrary to their own opinions.

Environmental friendly products

We ultimately cultivate vegetables to feed ourselves, and we therefore want to remove the competition in an environmentally friendly way. But what do we mean by an environmentally friendly product? Is it a product which is kind to the environment or improves it? In my view it is a product which affects the environment as little as possible. But how do you know if a product is environmentally friendly these days? Is there clear information stated on the packaging so that you can compare the ingredients of one pesticide with another and choose the one which is least harmful?

You should not plant out these cauliflowers. The club root is already visible.

Active and non-active ingredients

The name of the substance that does the job, known as the active ingredient, is always stated on the packaging. Often that active ingredient is not present in a pure form, but it is contaminated with toxic materials. Also, additives such as colours and scents, solvents and propellants are often added to the product. There is rarely any information on the packaging about these substances, the non-active ingredients in a product, although it is well known that they can be very harmful.

It is said that a bicycle rim round the cabbage will deter pigeons. The rest of the cabbage is protected by netting.

Bio or eco?

Various garden centres sell ready-made organic products and the brand name of these products often includes "bio", "eco" or "natural". Sometimes this is deserved, but sometimes it is not. For example there is a liquid insecticide Pynosect whose vegetable-based active ingredient Pyrethrum is broken down within two days by sunlight.

Pyrethrum has only one disadvantage: it does not work selectively. That is to say, it doesn't only kill one type of creature, but a whole group. Now the chemical poperonylbutoxide is added to the product to make it stronger. This substance inhibits the removal of other chemicals from the human body and it is not entirely clear whether it is carcinogenic or not. Nevertheless Pyrethrum and Spruzit packaging regularly says: purely vegetable in origin. You must therefore always ask if Pyrethrum is mixed with piperonylbutoxide.

However attractive Colorado beetles may be, both the adult specimens and the larvae are extremely greedy. Pull them off by hand.

The fact that a product is vegetable in origin does not always mean that it is not harmful to the environment, or that it is not poisonous. Hence there is the apparently environmentally friendly insecticide Derris, which contains the active ingredient Rotenon. Even though this substance is vegetable in origin and easily biodegradable, it is extremely poisonous to pigs and fish.

A whole colony of aphids on rape. There is no point in fighting them at this stage. Remove the plant or cut away part of it.

Make your own pesticides

So you see that there are disadvantages associated with many pesticides, whether they are of chemical or vegetable origin. But you do not always need these treatments by any means, since home-made remedies often work very well against pests and diseases.

Stinging nettle extract

Stinging nettle extract: pick a good bunch of stinging nettles and leave them to stand in a bucket for 24-36 hours. After straining the extract, dilute it by a factor of 2 to 10 and spray over the affected plants. The degree of dilution depends on the plant and the insect you are trying to eliminate. You can use stinging nettle extract against all kinds of insects, including aphids. In most cases you will need to spray repeatedly.

TIP

BIO-S, S.P.S. Hepar sulphuris and sulphur are all tried and tested biological remedies against fungus, rust and scab. You can also dust with basalt meal and coral chalk as a precautionary measure, since both dry out fungi and insects.

Slugs and snails   If slugs and snails are the enemy, take small jars containing a little beer and bury them in the ground up to the rim around the affected plants. Slugs and snails happen to be very fond of beer, and they will approach the jars and drown in the liquid.

The larva of the onion fly shrivels and kills young plants.

Flies as pests   Carrot, leek, onion and cabbage flies can be kept off with anti-insect netting, while carrot and cabbage flies can also be kept down using tansy powder. Use 1 gramme of powder per square metre. The larva of the cabbage fly will not stand a chance if you apply a cabbage collar around the neck of the cabbage plant root. You can keep the larva of the onion fly well away from your onions by alternating the onions with rows of carrots. This is also a way of keeping the carrot fly away from your carrots. Comment: due to its fine structure, anti-insect netting also keeps some light off the plants. If you want the growth of these covered plants to keep pace with the uncovered plants, you must sow the covered plants earlier.

Camomile tea   In order to fight against fungus, you can use a pot of camomile tea. Soak 5 grammes of dried camomile or 10 grammes of fresh camomile in a litre of water for a day. Moisten the seed with the extract and also the young seedlings after germination.

Left: sowing underground clover will prevent caterpillars from eating your cabbage.

In order to make young plants more resistant to fungal diseases, you can spray them with horsetail tea. Boil 30 grammes of dried field

A cabbage collar made of asphalt paper or roofing felt will make sure the cabbage fly cannot lay her eggs on the cabbage plant.

87

horsetail (equisetum arvense) in a litre of water. Let it steep for at least 24 hours, and then dilute the extract with water (1 part extract to 4 parts of water). Stir well and spray. The treatment is particularly effective if you spray before the disease becomes evident and repeat once every three weeks.

Soil-dwelling insects

Soil-dwelling insects such as leatherjackets and cockchafer grubs can be treated to a mixture of sawdust, bran and molasses or treacle. Mix it up well and sprinkle it between the plants in the evenings.
This mixture lies so heavy on the insects' stomachs that they can hardly move. The creatures are then easy prey for birds. All soil-dwelling insects are attracted by fresh green material in the soil, so you should never dig fresh green manure under.

Whitefly

African marigolds and nasturtiums give off certain substances which make the neighbouring plants which absorb these substances less attractive to whitefly. Sow these plants near tomatoes, cucumbers and gherkins.

Eelworms

Root, stalk and leaf eelworms also sometimes occur. A varied crop rotation system is very helpful in these cases. You should also plant African marigolds in places where eelworm infestation has taken place. Tagetes tenuifolia is the most effective variety.

TIP
Since the carrot fly flies very low, you can keep it off by erecting a 65 cm high screen of plastic sheeting around the carrot bed. The carrots will get sufficient light and it is cheap too.

Fruit rot in raspberries will spread very quickly in moist conditions. Make sure the wind can blow through the plants.

Flea beetles   Flea beetles are actually small beetles which are formidable jumpers. They can completely spoil a harvest of turnip tops and radishes. Keep the soil moist, since they hate this. You can also alternate the rows with garden cress. Flea beetles are so fond of garden cress that they will leave the radishes and turnip tops alone. But you can also catch them. Smear a plank with treacle, glue or wallpaper adhesive (actually anything sticky will do) and wave it above the plant. The flea beetles will jump up and stick to it.

The small-flowered African marigold, Tagetes tenuifolia, *is charming to see and effectively purifies the soil.*

Mice   Mice cause quite different problems. Give the mice alternative mice pellets: mix 3 parts flour with 1 part chalk and 1 part sugar. Mix it all together with enough water to form a paste.
Let the paste dry out and crumble the resulting mass once it has hardened.

Absinthe tea   Absinthe tea is very effective for controlling various insects and snails. Boil 100 grammes of wormwood in one litre of water. Let the mixture stand for 24 hours, strain it and spray it undiluted over the plants. Unless specified to the contrary, you should repeat treatments with home-made products once a week.

Next page: this black-bird has got it in for your currant harvest.

You can add two percent of soft soap to all liquid pesticides. The soap allows the medium to flow better and also helps it to adhere.

Pruning fruit

Have you ever seen a kitchen garden

without fruit?
I certainly have not.
There are always a
couple of bushes of
berries or currants.

In this chapter I will tell you how to

maintain and prune these fruit bushes.

Before producing their tasty fruits, many fruit trees bear splendid blossom.

Small fruits are not only tasty but they are also useful since they can act as a windbreak. Apple and pear trees are now also being grown as hedging fruit trees and windbreaks. A solitary plum or peach tree improves the silhouette and adds height to the often rather "flat" kitchen garden.

There are probably as many pruning methods as there are gardeners. Try to find out what type of wood bears flowers or fruit on the bush or tree, how fast it grows and whether the fruit needs a long or short time to ripen. If you know all that, then pruning is no longer as difficult. It is almost always important to allow the sunlight to penetrate the heart of the bush or tree, both to improve the size and ripening of the fruit and to keep the plant healthy.

Blackcurrants

Blackcurrants bear fruit on the youngest wood and they can be pruned from November to March. Before the buds open in the spring they swell up quite large. If you are even a little bit late with pruning you are likely to break too many buds off the branches. It is therefore wisest to prune in November.
In order to get a well-shaped bush you should prune the branches on the young bush (often only one or two branches) above an eye facing the outside of the bush. The strongest branches grow from these eyes – facing from the heart towards the outside of the bush. Four or five

Cut out the older, darker wood from blackcurrants. The newly-formed shoots, which are much lighter in colour, are left behind.

branches with lateral twigs may develop. You should not let these framework branches grow to more than three years old. Each year you should prune away all worn-out branches growing on the framework branches as deep as possible. The new shoots pointing towards the outside of the bush should be left. This will produce an attractively shaped bush in which the light can penetrate right to the heart. The young branches of the blackcurrant are recognisable by the light colour of the wood.

Raspberries   On the common summer-fruiting raspberry, prune all fruit-bearing branches right back to the ground immediately after harvesting. If you forgot to do this then you can still do it in the spring without causing any damage. The stems formed in the previous growing season should be left, since they will bear fruit next year. If you grow raspberries along wires, do not allow more than seven stems to remain per running metre. The surplus young stems can also be cut away now. The autumn raspberry bears fruit on branches which appeared in the same year. Keep 10-12 shoots per running metre on this type of raspberry in the new year. Leave the thickest stems on both varieties of raspberry, since they will bear the most and the best fruit.

Blackberries   The blackberry is rather like the raspberry in that it also flowers on young wood and has long branches which are bound. Remove the

T I P

If you find it difficult to distinguish worn-out and new wood on a blackcurrant, it is best to harvest them branch and all (and pull the berries off the branch somewhere else). Then you have pruned the shrub as well.

The young "Gieser Wildeman" pear is being trained along a fence here. The pear will therefore not create as much shade. (Huis Bingerden)

worn out and dead wood in October. Do not tie the young branches yet because they are sensitive to frost. It is better to bend them down to the ground and cover them with leaves, straw or an old rush mat. This will allow the bush to survive the winter unharmed. After the winter you can then tie the branches of thorny varieties at a distance of 30 cm using wire: a distance of 15 cm is sufficient for the thornless blackberry.

Prune the old fruit-bearing branches down to the ground and then thin out the bushes again; do not leave more than seven branches per running metre.

Japanese wineberries

The Japanese wineberry also bears fruit on its youngest branches and should be pruned and, if necessary, tied just like the thornless blackberry.

Currants

Currants, the family which includes red and white currants, bear fruit on perennial or older branches. You should not prune until February or March. The guideline when pruning is that the light must be able to penetrate the bush. Each year you should therefore prune a few of the very oldest branches back as deep as possible. As a rule, however, only cut away the young primary shoots. Occasionally a young shoot can be left to replace an old framework branch. There should be a maximum of five framework branches on a bush.

The best currants grow on small annual branches growing out from a main branch. These branches (10cm or at the most 20cm long) are left when pruning. Shorten long lateral branches to 1cm. When red-

Keep young, long, new shoots which are formed on older wood low in the bush or come up almost from ground level.

currants are grown as a hedge they get more light. Keep to three stems per running metre. Note: fruit bushes or trees should be pruned shorter (deep) or longer (little), depending on how vigorously they grow.

Raspberries are among the soft fruits Pick the ripe fruit each day. Overripe fruit attracts bees and wasps and increases the chance of fruit rot.

Gooseberries   Gooseberries bear on both young and perennial wood. In early March you should remove all lateral wood back to a height of 40cm, and you should leave seven framework branches. The remaining lateral branches should be thinned out to a distance of 10 cm apart, remembering that the sturdiest branches yield the biggest fruit. Lateral branches which grow downwards and inwards should be cut back deepest. Plants which suffer from mildew in the summer should have all their branches cut back during the winter. Unfortunately the bush will lose some fruiting wood as a result. Do not give too much fertiliser to gooseberries which are sensitive to mildew, since that helps the disease to gain a foothold.

Grapes   The grape carries fruit on side shoots, on wood at least a year old. This plant is usually grown fanned out or wired against a wall or fence. If you want to achieve a shape like this you should cut the young plant, which often consists of a single branch, back to 1 metre high after planting. The best time for pruning is November/December, because then the plant is resting. If you prune in the spring, when the sap has started flowing again, the wounds will begin to bleed, and this

T I P

The branches of a gooseberry bush have a strong tendency to grow towards the ground. Take this into account when pruning and shaping the bush by pruning the framework branches back to an inward-facing eye.

95

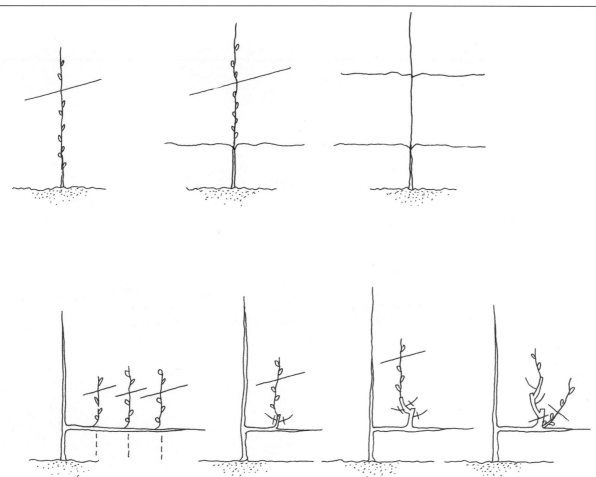

Left: the redcurrant bears fruit on old wood. Do not leave too much old wood, so that enough light will reach the berries.

bleeding is almost impossible to staunch. The eyes below the pruning will run out, and you should tie down one or more shoots as framework branches (known as laterals) depending on the shape (loop or fan). The following year side-shoots will appear on these laterals, and these will bear fruit. Cut the twigs which have borne fruit each year above 2-5 eyes (depending on the variety). If an excessively large pruning knob develops over the years, you can remove it in December, except for one branch with several eyes. Bunches of grapes will grow from the buds which run out. Leave the first two bunches and break off the other shoots along with their small bunches of fruit if applicable. You need not be afraid that the plant will begin to bleed during this little job, since the shoots are still green and not yet woody. The shoots do not grow very long, so break the fruit-bearing shoots off at the second leaf above the last bunch. You should also break off the side-shoots which develop. This allows the sun to shine on the bunches, which will improve the sugar content of the grapes and give the fruit a better colour. You can thin out the bunch of grapes if necessary.

Winter pruning of grapes.

Train berries along a wire so that they will have more light. Do not tie on more than three framework branches per running metre.

Stone fruits   The best time to prune cherries, morellos, plums and peaches is immediately after harvesting, because the wounds will then heal easily. If you prune in the winter, during the dormant season, the wounds will stay open a long time and diseases can enter the plant. Pruning is not advisable in the spring either, because the flow of sap in

Above left: long leafy shoots are broken off to the second leaf after the bunch of grapes. Above: the result is that more sunlight can reach the bunches.

Above right: you can completely break off side shoots which have no grapes growing on them. Below: the result is that it is easier for the bunches to catch the sunlight. This is essential for colouring and sugar formation.

stone fruits is again too strong. The bushes have a tendency to bleed and gum and wounds must be avoided at all costs.

Plums   Plums bear fruit on both young and older wood. Pruning should therefore be limited to removing dead wood and thinning out the excess fruiting wood, so that enough light can penetrate to the heart of the tree. Branches which do not get enough (sun)light will easily die off. It is therefore occasionally necessary to prune a few branches from the top of the tree. Always cover the pruning wounds with wound sealant or latex on stone fruit.

Morellos   Morellos bear fruit almost exclusively on one-year-old branches growing on the outside of the tree. The older wood often stays completely bare. You should therefore, cut away all young and worn out wood as deep as possible right from the youth of the plant. This will stimulate the growth of fruiting wood and keep the size of the tree down.

Peaches   Peaches also yield their best fruit on the last year's wood. As with the morello, the older wood has a tendency to become bare. Deep replacement pruning is necessary in September – this really must not be earlier or later. Snip off the worn-out branches flat above a vigorous new shoot. Since peaches bleed very easily, you should try to prevent cutting into thick wood.

Peaches also bear fruit on young wood. Prune the tree immediately after harvesting.

Preserving and storing

If you have a good growing plan, you can eat home-grown vegetables almost all the year round. Since January and February are difficult months for gardening, it is worth knowing rather more about various storage methods.

In this book we have placed the emphasis on "live" storage. This old-fashioned method has proven very successful in the past and, apart from a little trouble, this environmentally friendly storage method will not cost you a penny.

Completely dry onions can be stored in nets or jute sacks in a cool, dry room.

Leafy vegetables

Curly kale, Brussels sprouts, chicory, winter lettuce, lamb's lettuce and sorrel are completely hardy and can simply be left in the ground. Remove the outside leaves from other cabbage varieties, and then hang them upside-down in a cool but frost-free place. The advantage of this method is that there is only a very small chance of rot and blemishes. On the minus side, however, there will be some weight loss. You can also cut the cabbages from the stem with a few of their outer leaves and stack them in a dry, cool place with relatively high air humidity. The cabbages must be turned regularly and you must cut away any decayed parts with a sharp knife.

Store carrots and beets dirty

Carrots and beets can be stored in the garden frost-free if you pile them up in a heap or store them in a pit, covered with a layer of soil and perhaps some wheat straw (see further on in the text under silage). You can do this indoors by storing them in a box. Carrots and beets should be stored dirty, that is to say the foliage should be removed, but the soil residues should be left on the roots. Potatoes, shallots and onions must be left in the ground until the leaves are

TIP

A drainage tube or plastic pipe in the middle of the silage pit provides good ventilation. The end sticks out above the hole and should be sealed off with cotton wool or balls of newspaper during frosty periods!

dead. You should store them in a dark, cool and well-ventilated place. Celeriac can also be stored here once its foliage has been removed. Particularly in the case of onions and shallots you should make sure that the storage area is cool enough, because with a little warmth and moisture they will begin to shoot. Onions and shallots which have dried on the ground can also be bound in strings and hung up.

You can harvest onion bulbs when the foliage begins to break off and two-thirds of it has turned yellow.

Dry beans can be dried in the pod and then shucked (peeled). They are then dried out and can be stored in airy bags.
Salsify, Jerusalem artichokes, leeks, parsnips and winter carrots can be left on the ground, but winter carrots should be covered with a thick layer of straw. Winter carrots, like winter radishes and winter beet, can also be stored using silage methods.

Silage   Dig a hole in the ground, cover the bottom with a layer of straw 10 cm thick and place the vegetables and soil inside. Spread some sand around the vegetables to prevent drying out. Finally place another layer of straw over the top. In severe winters lay a sheet of plastic on top of the straw and then a layer of soil on top of that. Dig up the soil for this layer from around the pit, to create a channel. This will serve to catch and drain away the rainwater. Hardy plants can be stored by the silage method on wet clay soils where plants cannot be harvested from the frozen soil.

TIP

If you are afraid of mice getting into or among your ensiled vegetables, remember that these creatures hate the smell of onions and mint. Chop a few onions among the ensiled vegetables or scatter a few leaves of mint among the heap or pit.

On wet soils with a high groundwater level, you should store vegetables in a heap on the ground rather than in a pit.

Drying

If you think that these methods date back to the time of your ancestors, you are quite right. The method is described here because a natural drying method costs nothing and above all no preservatives are added. You will only retain 10 to 20% of the original weight – this may be a disadvantage, but you should consider that it might be more convenient when large amounts are involved.

The ideal climate

A typical British problem is that we do not have an ideal climate for drying. If you want to use the natural drying method, you will need a continuous period of sunshine lasting 5-14 days (depending on the type of product), plenty of warmth, low air humidity level and some wind. This is not always easy in Britain: you may get the wind, but warmth is a different matter...!

The ideal drying temperature is between 30 and 45° C. In glorious weather and a slight breeze you can leave many products to dry in a lightly shaded place (a carport?).
A cold frame provides rather more certainty. You can create a favourable drying climate in a cold frame by leaving the glass in position above the products being dried, but removing a window on each side

TIP

Never leave any "living" matter in direct sunlight to dry. It will dry out, but the colour and a lot of the flavour will be lost. The same applies to dried flowers, herbs and the like.

Pull the onions out of the soil and leave them on the ground to dry for a few days.

An upturned pallet with some chicken wire is ideal for quick drying.

of the glass. This will provide the necessary ventilation. Granted, drying in the oven is more convenient and reliable in practice, but only if you can ensure that the temperature will not exceed 45°C. Leave the oven door slightly open to allow the air to circulate.

Dry, well-ventilated attics are of course also excellent natural drying places, but you must be sure to keep the dust away from the products or goods you are drying.

Salt to prevent discoloration

In principle you can dry all vegetables and fruit, but apples and sweet pears are by far the most suitable products for drying. Peel the fruit and remove the cores.

Cut them into sections or rings and immediately place them in plenty of water with some salt to prevent discoloration. You should allow about 50 grammes of salt for 4.5 litres of water. After the fruit has drip-dried, thread a piece of string through the apple rings, keeping them separate, and hang them on a clothes line to dry. Impale the apple pieces on sticks and lay them in the oven, supported by a lath. A stand for the pieces to allow you to dry them above a radiator is perhaps even more convenient. The drying is much more gradual and will not require any extra energy. The best way of drying pear pieces and many types of vegetables is on drying frames consisting of a wooden frame with cheese cloth or netting stretched over it. The frames should be large enough to fit on the oven shelf.

TIP

French beans and mushrooms can be dried successfully in the oven, but you must blanch them well first. Boiling or steaming vegetables is necessary in order to kill the enzymes which are responsible for the ageing process in the harvested products.

103

Drying herbs Tie herbs in small bunches and hang them out to dry upside down on the clothes line. Do not forget that they should not be dried in direct sunlight. Place small boxes or other containers under herbs from which you want to harvest the seed, so that they will catch the seeds.

The dried product has kept its "living" colour.

TIP

Bundle the herbs together with elastic bands. When drying the bunch will shrink and become smaller. The elastic shrinks with the bunch so that the stalks do not fall out.

Of course herbs can also be dried in the other places mentioned, or near a central heating boiler, but always take steps to keep out the dust, for example by wrapping each bunch in paper. This also acts as a screen against the sunshine. It is best not to use newspaper, because newsprint contains toxic toluene, which should be kept off the herbs. If you do not have any of the drying options referred to above and it is raining outside, you can dry herbs in the microwave for a few minutes. Herbs and vegetables are brittle to touch when they are dry. Fruit is dry when no more juice comes out when you pinch it. Stack the dried products loosely in tins or glass jars and store them in the dark.

Pasteurising fruit That one harvest of cherries which you have saved from the birds with great difficulty is worth storing. The best way to do this is by using alcohol or by pasteurising the fruit. Here we will only consider pasteurising.

If you heat the contents of preserving jars and pots with twist-off lids long enough at around 80°C, most bacteria will be destroyed.

Left: herbs preserved in oil or vinegar can stand in the sun.

105

Air will escape from the jars during heating and water vapour will collect inside. When cooled this steam again turns into water, which creates a vacuum inside the pot. Do not bottle meat or vegetables, because there is a specific bacteria (Clostridium botulinum) which grows very well in such airless conditions. You cannot see it, because does not change the appearance of the food, but they give off a toxin which can cause serious food poisoning when eaten. What is more the pot lids do not come off. Also you cannot smell or taste the rot. You can bottle fruit and vegetables in syrup or vinegar, since the bacteria mentioned above cannot grow under sweet or acid conditions.

What must you do and avoid?

Always observe the following rules:

- clean the jars with hot soda water, rinse them out with hot water and leave them to drip-dry on a clean cloth
- boil (twist-off) lids in soda water for 5 minutes, rinse them and let them drip-dry on a clean cloth
- fill the jars up to 2 cm below the rim and add syrup (150-300 grammes per litre) up to the level of the fruit
- clean the rim of the pot and screw on the (twist-off) lid firmly
- put the jars in a pan on a cloth folded double or on a grid; fill the pan (until the jars are almost covered) with water at the same temperature as the contents of the jars.
- the bottling time begins when the water has reached the correct temperature
- take the jars out of the pan immediately after pasteurising and put them on a shelf or cloth; cover them with a tea towel to prevent the jars cracking in the draught
- store the jars in a dark, cool, dry place.

Fruit juice

You can make excellent juice from juicy fruits like berries, plums and the like, and also from slightly damaged fruit. You should try it! The photographs on page 109 tell you exactly how to go about it.

TIP

Jars of herbs can be stored in a spice rack in the kitchen, but only if the herbs are kept in tins, or jars with dark-coloured glass. This is the best way to preserve the quality of the product.

1   If you want to dry herbs in the microwave, clean them
    first.

2   It is important to dab dry the herbs properly.

3   Place the herbs to be dried close together on a few sheets of
    kitchen roll.

4   Cover the herbs with a few layers of kitchen paper.

5   Place the package on a grille and cover it with a plate so
    that the paper will not "flap about".

6   Three minutes at 600 watts is enough for most herbs.

1. For cherries in juice, first remove the stalks and wash the fruit. Fill the pan with enough water to just cover the cherries. Add sugar to taste. 2. Meanwhile, wash the jars and (twist-off) lids in hot soda water. Rinse with hot water and leave them to drip dry on a clean tea towel. Put the pan of fruit on the heat and bring to the boil.

3. Let the cherries, water and sugar boil for a while. 4. Fill the jars with cherries and add enough juice to cover the cherries – cherries which are above the juice will be discoloured. 5. Seal the jars and leave them to cool upside down. Since you can never be sure that all the air was kept out of the jar, the contents can only be kept for a limited time.

Extras in the kitchen garden

Reading this title you may think: surely extras are unnecessary? But then if I do have some space left over... Nothing could be less true – these extras are important in an organic kitchen garden. We are talking about herbs, perennial and annual plants and cut flowers.

Herbs in the kitchen garden

Herbs are mainly used to improve the flavour and taste of food. They are usually also beneficial to the digestion. Correct use of herbs can improve health, thereby building up a greater resistance to illness.

In the garden, herbs attract various different groups of insects. Some of these are necessary for cross-pollination, while other, harmful, insects can be kept at bay by herbs. You can also make remedies from herbs to protect plants against pests and diseases. Even for this single reason it is very worthwhile to set aside some room for selected herbs in your kitchen garden.

The best location

Herbs will actually grow well on any soil, although the disadvantage of clay soil is that the plants will be much less aromatic. A sheltered, sunny location is best suited to herbs and they should, of course, be as close to the kitchen as possible.

The soil should not be too damp and, above all, not acidic: a calcium-rich, sandy soil is best for herbs. The greyer and more needle-shaped the herb leaf is, the more dry, sunshine and warmth it will need. A low-lying site, where the soil stays cold for a long time is therefore the worst possible location.

If the whole garden is low-lying, the only solution is to raise the part

An archway in the beech hedge leading into the kitchen garden should be wide enough to allow a wheelbarrow through easily.

Here you can find herbs, annuals, roses and vegetables all together in this old-fashioned kitchen garden.

110

where you are going to grow herbs. Make sure that the high side is to the north so that the herbs can grow on the south-facing slope.

Special treatment   You should remember that certain herbs such as mint (all varieties) can spread out enormously. Bury them in large pots or bottomless buckets so that the root growth stays within the limits. Horseradish has large leaves and therefore takes up a lot of space. If you dig up this plant and leave even one tiny piece of root in the ground, you will very soon have an enormous plant again. I would therefore also consign this plant to a large bucket. Other taller herbs, such as annual borage (cucumber weed), annual dill, lovage, tarragon and Roman chervil can also be used as windbreaks for other lower-growing herbs and vegetables.

It is best to uproot and divide perennial herbs (all the varieties referred to in this book unless indicated otherwise) once every three or four years, in the spring or autumn. Throw the innermost, oldest parts of the plant on the compost heap and then replant the younger parts.

Sow or buy   Many herbs are perennials. They can be grown from seed, but it is usually simpler and cheaper to buy them from a garden centre. If you are cultivating the plants exclusively for your own use in the kitchen, you will only need a few of each variety, while packets usually contain

Thyme needs plenty of sunshine, warmth and dry conditions.

An ornamental comfrey. The root of the original comfrey, Symphytum officinale, was and still is used to heal wounds and relieve pain.

hundreds of seeds. The situation is rather different if your herbs are intended for use as part of your combined growing scheme.

Herbs like a sunny, sheltered position (Huis Bingerden).

Since the sowing times and growth conditions of different herbs vary tremendously, it is important to follow the growing instructions on the seed packets very carefully.

Combinations with herbs   The following combinations of vegetables and herbs are very successful and often yield specific benefits.

Horseradish between potatoes: increases potato yield. Garden peppers (annual) with radishes: prevents flea beetles in the radishes. Lettuce with chervil (annual): creates healthy heads of lettuce without aphids.
Borage (annual) with tomatoes: the herb creates "air traffic" (bumble bees) among the tomatoes, so that the first flowers on the tomato will all bear fruit. Borage should be planted just outside the greenhouse, then the herb will keep the bumble bees and other bees out of the greenhouse.
Camomile (annual) and African marigolds between onions: prevents attacks by onion fly; a good preventative measure against aphids.
Dill (annual) in a single row between rows of broad beans: keeps bean fly off the broad beans: the dill will be affected instead.

TIP
You can plant the cold north side of a patch of raised ground with evergreen shrubs such as *Buxus sempervirens* (small box tree) and *Lonicera nitida* (Poor man's box). These will provide shelter all the year round.

Hyssop, sage and thyme between cabbages: butterflies (and, therefore, caterpillars) do not like these strong-smelling herbs. Snails don't like them either.

Celery (annual) between cabbage: prevents rust attacking the celery and protects the cabbage against all kinds of insects.

Celery with camomile (annual): prevents leek fly from attacking leek plants.

The smell of sage keeps butterflies (and hence caterpillars) well away from the cabbages.

Cut flowers in the vegetable garden

If you are planning to plant a corner or strip of your kitchen garden with perennial plants, you should remember that they cannot be used in your crop rotation plan. Perennial plants, as the name suggests, have to stay in the same place for a number of years. You should therefore consider reserving a wide strip in the middle of the kitchen garden for cut flowers. The surrounding vegetable plants will benefit from this floral company because the flowers attract many useful insects. These improve pollination and consume other, more harmful insects. If you have decided to grow cut flowers, you should loosen the soil that you are going to use and only manure lightly. Compost will be best in this case, since most of the cut flowers named below do not like fresh farmyard manure. Many of these plants are related to herbs which generally do not like heavy applications of fertiliser since the likelihood of disease and uncontrolled growth increases drastically under nutrient-rich conditions.

TIP

Mint varieties, Roman chervil, chives, lady's bedstraw, lovage or sea parsley plants are all perennial herbs which can survive in semi-shade. Annual parsley, celery and chervil are content with rather less sunshine.

113

Plants in pots can be planted out later in the season

The pollen in perennial plants spreads very widely over a few years. As with herbs, you must uproot the plants once every three or four years, divide them and replant them. The plants are almost always sold in pots by growers, so you can plant them well into the season without causing root damage or arresting their growth (they will need watering in dry periods).

This herb garden gets quite a bit of shade. Parsley, celery, chervil, chives, mint and lovage will all be satisfied with this location.

Suitable perennials for cutting

Name	Height in cm	Flowering-month	Colour	Comments
Achillea taygetea (Yellow yarrow)	50	6-9	yellow	grey leaves
Aconium carmichaelii (Monkshood)	70	8-9	blue	fairly sunny position
Aconitum napellus (Common monkshood)	100	7-10	blue	fairly sunny position
Alchemilla mollis (Lady's mantle)	40	5-8	yellow	flowers continously - also thrives in light shade
Artemisia ludoviciana (Wormwood)	80	-	-	attractive grey leaf
Aster "Silver Queen" *Aster laterifolius* "Horizontalis"	80	8-10	purple-white	small flowers also in light shade

Following page: angelica is a decorative biennial herb for semi-shade. The seeds can be used as an alternative sweetener. "Liqueur des Anges" is also well worth trying.

Honesty (Lunaria redivia) is a perennial plant which carries separate "pennies" and can also cope well with shade.

Name	Height in cm	Flowering-month	Colour	Comments
Aster multiflorus "Monte Casino"	100	9-11	white	small flowers, also thrives in light shade
Astrantia major (Masterwort)	50	6-9	white-pink	damp position, also light shade
Buphthalmum salicifolium (Yellow ox-eye daisy)	50	7-8	yellow	
Campanula lactiflora (Bellflower)	90	6-8	light blue	light shade and moist position
Chelone obliqua (Turtle head)	90	6-9	lilac-pink	light shade
Chrysanthemum maximum "Silver Princess" (Marguerite)	40	6-9	white	light shade and rich soil
Chrysanthemum rubellum "Clara Curtis"	80	8-10	pink	light shade and rich soil
Echinops ritro (Globe thistle)	100	7-9	blue	
Helenium "Moerheim Beauty" (Sneezeweed)	100	7-9	red-brown	
Humulus lupulus (Hop)	300	8-9	greenish yellow	bears hop bells
Lysimachia clethroides (Loosestrife)	70	7-9	white	also thrives in the shade
Monarda didyma "Cambridge Scarlet" (Bergamot, also Oswego tea)	80	7-8	red	light shade and damp position
Physostegia virginiana "Summer snow" (Obedient plant)	70	7-10	white	rich soil, also light shade
Rudbeckia sullivantii "Goldsturm" (Coneflower)	60	7-10	yellow with dark heart	
Salvia superba "Mainacht" (Salvia)	50	5-8	blue-purple	
Sidalcea "Elsie Hugh"	80	6-8	satin pink	
Solidaster x luteus	60	7-9	yellow	cross between Aster and Solidago

Catnip, which attracts many useful insects and also cats, is also reasonable as a cut flower.

The angelica flower is ball-shaped. If the seeds have just formed (as shown here), it is best to wrap the umbel in cellophane pricked through with small holes. This will catch the ripe seeds.

TIP

On light, warm soils, the best time for planting is September/October. This will give the plants sufficient opportunity to become established for the winter. On heavy, cold soils it is better to plant in the spring.

If you plant in groups of at least three of each type, there will be some flowers worth picking later on.

Annuals   The advantage of annual cut flowers is that they can fit in nicely with the crop rotation plan. The rows of vegetables can be alternated with rows of cut flowers. Of course you can also choose a separate area for cut flowers. Annual cut flowers also offer the same benefits as cut flowers which are used as perennials: they attract useful insects and fill up your vases.

Moisten the soil before you begin to sow. Make a number of gullies in the ground and sow the seeds in them as thinly as possible. Then cover the thicker seeds with a layer of sand and the finest seeds can simply be mixed in with the surface of the soil by raking the top layer very gently. Moisten the ground again after sowing and then press it down.

To prevent drying out, cover the rows with jute, rush matting or black plastic. This will also prevent the birds from stealing any seeds. When the seeds germinate, remove the covering and spray regularly during long dry periods.

Yarrow is an old-fashioned perennial plant, whose flowers are suitable for drying.

This is also yarrow. The plant is a result of cross-fertilisation in the kitchen garden and looks like an Achillea millefolium.

Annuals which are sown directly outside	Name	Sowing time	Height in cm	distance between the plants in cm	Colour
	Agrostemma githago "Purple Queen" (Corn cockle)	mid-April	80	25	purple-pink

The fine seeds of annual plants are almost always mixed with moist river sand for good distribution. Sowing too close together gives poor results. If you have sown too close together you must thin out – a nice little job for a rainy day.

The distance that should be maintained between the plants depends on the variety. You can plant out the uprooted plants somewhere else if required, although this does not apply to plants with a taproot.

Name	Sowing time	Height in cm	distance between the plants in cm	Colour
Agrostis nebulosa (cloud-grass)	late April	40	20	n/a
Anethum graveolens (Dill)	April-May	120	45	yellow
Antirrhinum majus "Tip Top" (Larger snapdragon)	April	80	25	mixed
Atriplex hortensis "Rubra" (Grey sage brush)	late April	120	30	red-purple
Calendula officinalis "Radio" (Marigold)	April	60	20	orange
Centaurea cyanus "Blue Ball" (Cornflower)	April	80	15	blue
Chrysanthemum carinatum (Painted daisy)	April	60	25	mixed
Coix-lacrima-jobi (Job's tears)	late April	70	10	n/a
Coreopsis tinctoria "Carmen" (Tickseed)	April	50	25	warm red
Cosmea bipinnata	late April	120	335	mixed
Delphinium consolida (Larkspur)	April	100	25	mixed

Golden rod is an excellent cut flower. It's a pity that the plant suffers from mildew later in the year. Try the shorter varieties, which seem to be less severely affected.

Zinnias come in nearly every colour and size.

Tithonia rotundifolia *"Goldfinger" is not a commonplace annual. It flowers for a very long time, but flowering begins very late if you sow it on location.*

Name	Sowing time	Height in cm	distance between the plants in cm	Colour
Dimorphoteca aurantiaca	late April	30	20	mixed
Euphorbia marginata (Snow on the mountain)	late April	60	35	white, variegated leaf
Gypsophila elegans (Gypsophila)	late April	60	35	white
Helianthus debilis cucumerifolius (miniature sunflower)				
Lagurus ovatus (Hare's tail grass)	late April	70	10	n/a
Lavatera trimestris "Silver Cup" (Mallow)	late April	80	35	silver-backed pink
Lathyrus odoratus (Sweet pea)	early April	150	15	mixed
Nicotiana alata "Limegreen" (ornamental tobacco)	May	60	30	greenish yellow
Nigella damascena "Miss Jekyll" (Love in a mist)	April	50	20	blue
Phacelia tanacetifolia	April	30	15	lavender-blue
Rudbeckia hirta "Goldflame" (Black-eyed Susan)	April	30	15	orange-yellow
Tanacetum parthenium "Balls White" (Bachelor's buttons)	late April	35	20	white
Tithonia rotundifolia (Round-leaved Mexican sunflower) yellow and orange	May	100	40	
Tropaeolum perigrinum (Canary creeper)	late April	200	25	yellow
Zinnia elegans "Early Wonder" (Zinnia)				

A little extra in the kitchen garden: pots and pans with "left-over" plants, from boxwood to succulents. Your old kitchen steps can be put to good use as well.

Following pages: The Heliops *is an old-fashioned cut flower. If you see the word* heli *(Greek for sun) in a Latin name, you can be sure that the plant in question needs a sunny site.*

Variations in the kitchen garden

Yes, you will be saying, there should be something to make the kitchen garden pleasing to the eye as well. The following chapter gives a number of ways of arranging your kitchen garden. Do you want a colourful garden or a fanciful design? Would you prefer a cottage garden, or classical style? The choice is yours.

A kitchen garden definitely does not have to be boring. It is true that most plants in the kitchen garden are roughly the same height and no vegetables grow in the winter. Still, bushes, climbers, colours and other materials can be used to transform your kitchen garden into a delightful place.

A red dahlia like this one goes beautifully with red Swiss chard or rhubarb with red stalks.

A decoratice vegetable garden at its best

This design has incorporated various vegetables which not only taste delicious but look attractive as well. We have tried to put together attractive combinations in which the plants are also technically suited to each other. The curved paths may seem surprising, but their shape provides an extra decorative element in the garden, while the tight beds are still easily accessible.

Scarlet runners, gold-coloured hops and white sweet peas are grown alongside the footpath on long sticks. The sticks are arranged in a circle and tied together at the top.

The garden is sheltered on three sides – only the south side has been left open. It is 15m long by 13m wide. The footpaths are 1m or 60cm wide and there are also paths 30cm wide between the 120 cm wide beds.

Right: "Romanesco" looks most like a cauliflower. This variety does not need to be covered, and it's much too beautiful anyway.

**Planting plan
Ornamental
vegetables in
colour:**

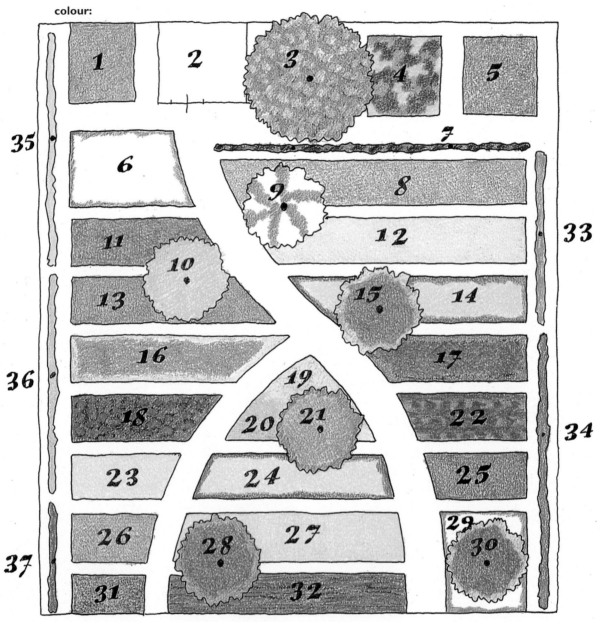

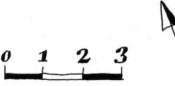

1 manure heap

2 shed

3 plums

4 compost heap with ornamental pumpkins

5 compost heap

6 white currants

7 blackcurrants trained along fences and wires

8 red cabbage

9 *Lathyrus odoratus* "Cuthbertson" (white annual
   sweet pea) along the edge and in the centre
   Matricaria chamomilla (annual camomile)

10 gold-coloured hop, *Humulus lupulus* 'Aureus'

11 medium height dahlias with brown-red leaves and red flowers, for example, *Dahlia* "Ellen Houston"

12 green cauliflower, for example. 'Romanesco'

13 artichoke, for example "Groene van Laon"

14 early spinach, later yellow tomatoes ("Golden Sunrise")

15 red-flowering scarlet runner beans along the edge and blanched celery inside

16 garden peas, later leeks

17 rhubarb with red stalks, for example, "Champagne Red"

18 strawberries with curly endives between

19 yellow variegated Salvia officinalis "Icterina"

20 yellow leaved Origanum vulgare (oregano) "Thumble's Variety" (this variety does not scorch in the sun)

21 gold-coloured hop along the edge and kitchen herbs inside - never combine celery with parsley

22 strawberries with red oakleaf lettuce in between

23 butter beans, for example, "Butterkönig"

24 first spinach, then yellow tomatoes and then leeks

25 Chinese cabbage

26 endive

27 butter beans

28 red-flowering scarlet runner beans along the edge and
blanched celery in the middle

29 Chinese chives

30 red-flowering scarlet runner beans along the edge and blanched celery in the middle

31 lettuce "Lollo Rosso"

32 early spinach, then red Swiss chard

33 sweet corn

34 marrowfat peas "Blauwschokker"

35 sweet corn

36 yellow raspberries

37 red raspberries

Rhubarb with red stems goes beautifully in the ornamental vegetable garden.

A fanciful kitchen This 13 x 13m kitchen garden includes cut flowers, fruit and herbs.
garden Sufficient path space has been created so that you can move around
easily. Apple trees pruned to palmleaf shape and a maple hedge
keep the wind off all year. Runner beans (west side), tomatoes and
Lathyrus (east side) fulfil this task during the summer.

In the centre of the garden there is a summer house where you can
take a rest when your labours are done. Flower pots are positioned on
the wide paths in such a way that they do not hinder access to the side
paths.

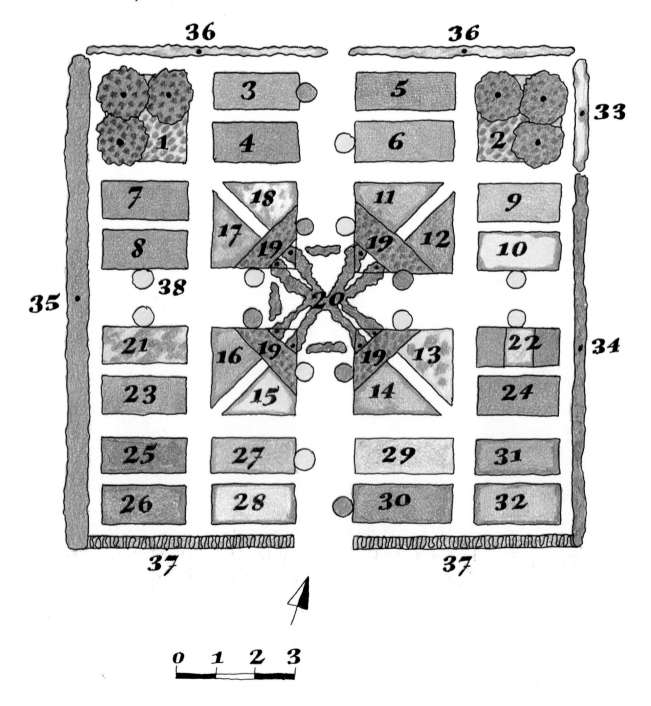

Arrangement of plants in the fanciful kitchen garden:

1. three blackcurrants and *Calendula officinalis* (marigold) in the foreground in the corner
2. three redcurrants and marigolds
3. oxheart cabbage, then curly kale
4. Swiss chard, for example "Gewone Groene" (Common Green), grown here for its young leaves
5. red cabbage
6. spinach "Breedblad Scherpzaad" (Broadleaved Sharpseed), lettuce in summer, for example, "Cindy"
7. Dwarf peas, later lamb's lettuce "Groene Volhart" (green full heart) (less sensitive to mildew in the winter)
8. Dwarf legumes and then endive for autumn cultivation
9. Chinese dwarf beans "Gitana"
10. butter beans
11. *Rudbeckia hirta* "Goldflame"
12. *Lavandula angustifolia* (lavender)
13. *Zinnia elegans* "Early Wonder"
14. *Nigella damascena* "Miss Jekyll) (Love in a mist)
15. *Matricaria chamomilla* (camomile)
16. *Dimorphoteca aurantiaca* (African daisy, Cape marigold)
17. *Salvia farinacea* "Victory " (annual blue Salvia, Mealy-cup sage)
18. *Callistephus chinensis* "Duchesse " (aster with chrysanthemum-type flowers) China aster
19. perpetual strawberries, such as "Baron Solemacher "
20. grape "Glorie van Boskoop " and /or *Humulus lupulus* (hop) and *Tropaeolum majus* (nasturtium) in the summer house
21. *Allium schoenoprasum* (chives) *Anthriscus cerefoliium* (annual chervil) and *Satureja montana* (Winter savoury)
22. *Petroselinum hortense* (Annual parsley) *Origanum vulgare* (Oregano) and *Artemisia dracunculus* (French tarragon)
23. early potatoes and horseradish
24. broad beans and later endive for autumn cultivation
25. medium high dahlias, such as the red dahlia ("Babylon ")
26. artichoke "Vroege Paarse" (Early Purple) (needs a lot of fertiliser)
27. carrots with onions
28. beets with chicory
29. leek with blanched celery
30. leek with carrots
31. beets with onion
32. sweet corn
33. *Helianthus annuus* (sunflower)
34. tomatoes, for example, "Allround" against woven screens of willow twigs, combined combination with *Lathyrus odoratus* (Sweet pea)
35. French beans on sticks
36. apple trees pruned to palmleaf shape
37. hedge of *Acer campestre* (field maple)
38. pots of *Canna indica* (Indian shot) *Ricinus communis* (Castor oil plant) and *Brugmansia* (Angels' trumpets)

If the summer is warm, sunny and dry, you can grow aubergines (eggplants) in the open. A jewel in your kitchen garden.

Summer asters come in many colours and they will go very well in a fanciful kitchen garden.

Following page: the Indian shot (Canna indica) has to be brought indoors during the winter. You can also keep the plant loose in pots and barrels, as has been done in the fanciful kitchen garden.

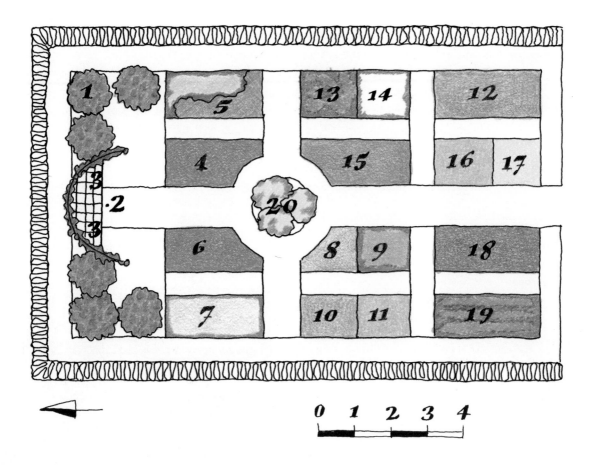

0   1   2   3   4

The cottage garden as a source of inspiration

The original cottage garden was above all an easy garden. Not too many fiddly things, easily accessible beds and easy paths. The cottage garden was truly functional: it was used to grow vegetables for eating and cut flowers to decorate the front room. This design (14.5 x 9.5m) maintains the principle of beds and small paths. The square and rectangular beds are easy to maintain. Gravel or cobblestones can be used for paving. It will be obvious that a hedge is needed on three sides. An old-fashioned privet hedge will do well around this cottage garden. The two main paths are both 1m wide, and the minor paths only 60cm.

Dahlias belong in a cottage garden.

Arrangement of plants in the cottage garden:

1   red and white currants
2   grape "Glorie van Boskoop" over the summer house
3   strawberries
4   lettuce varieties
5   dahlias and *Delphinium consolida* (Larkspur)
6   French beans
7   *Paeonia lactiflora* (Peony)
8   *Aquilegia vulgaris* (Common columbine)
9   carrots
10 *Callistephus chinensis* (China aster)

11 onions
12 dwarf marrowfat peas
13 Swiss chard
14 *Lilium regale* (lily)
15 beans
16 onions
17 *Chrysanthemum leucanthemum* "Maikönigin"
18 savoy cabbage
19 tomatoes
20 *Crambe maritima* (Sea kale) or *Angelica archangelica* (Angelica), or *Alcea rosea* (Hollyhock)

131

The functional garden

The space in this 7.5 x 14m back garden has been used very efficiently. Near the back door on the terrace there are movable boxes of herbs. The shed with bicycles and garden tools is therefore easily accessible. The gate at the back of the garden is reached by a paved footpath. All shelter is provided by fruit. The division from the neighbouring plot on the south is made up of decorative shrubs and berries. In the foreground there is plenty of space for decorative grasses and cut flowers and there is even room for the compost heap. The terrace consists of 60 x 40cm and 40 x 40cm paving stones.

Above right: the same kitchen garden looking southwards from under the plum tree.

Below right: the strawberry has had a place for centuries in the functional garden.

Arrangement of plants in the functional garden:

1 morello

2 "Queen Victoria" plum

3 "Conference" pear

4 "Glorie van Boskoop" grape

5 the ground under the apple tree is not cultivated; each year the soil here is covered with raw compost

6 *Buddleia davidii*

7 *Rosa pimpinellifolia* "Maigold" (botanical rose)

8 blackcurrant

9 redcurrant

10 *Chaenomeles japonica* (Japanese quince)

11 *Buddleia davidii* var. *nanhoensis*

12 *Perovskia atriplicifolia*

13 Rosa "New Dawn"

14 from the shed to the terrace

   5 tomato plants

   1 row of broccoli

   1 row of Swiss chard

   2 rows of French beans

   1 - 2 rows of perpetual strawberries

15 from the shed towards the gate:

   2 rows of runner beans with lettuce in between

   2 rows of broad beans with spinach in between

   1 row of kohlrabi

   1 row of onions

   1 row of carrots

16 a 25 cm high sleeper box with ornamental grasses

17 cut flowers

18 to 23 herbs with attractive flowers, for example, chives, thyme, marjoram, rosemary, lavender, sage, hyssop and mint

24 compost heap

The summer house in the centre of the kitchen garden offers shade and cool.

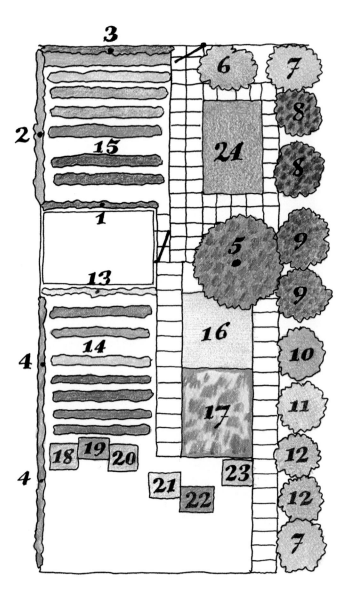

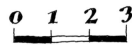

A classic kitchen garden

This is a plan for a traditional 20 x 15 m kitchen garden. You can see these gardens in many allotments.

If your kitchen garden is part of the garden behind your house the storage shed may be in another place and the compost heap will be out of sight somewhere at the back of the garden. The garden faces south-east and the north-west side is protected from the wind by the trees and bushes just behind the garden.

At the back of the garden there are large wooden compost and manure boxes and a storage shed, which also provide shelter. Part of the garden is also protected from strong winds on the north-west and north-east sides by the raspberry hedge, gooseberries and redcurrants and two plum trees. The plum "Opal" provides shade for the compost and manure boxes at midday.

Spread out beds

The beds are 120 cm wide, except the first two, which are 1m wide. The paths between the beds are 30 cm wide and just wide enough to walk along. The central path, however, is 1 m wide and the path running around the garden is 50 cm. The 240 x 150 cm cold frame can be used to nurture seeds and seedlings. You need the space around the frame for access. It is wise to mark and number the corner points of the beds so that you can follow the annual crop rotation scheme.

The delightful fruits of the edible Solanum muricatum "Pepino" taste of melon.

Special patterns of box were not used in the cottage gardens of long ago, but box was used to edge the beds. (Huis Bingerden)

Arrangement of plants in the classic kitchen garden:

A   storage shed
B   sifted compost
C   manure heap
D   conversion box
E   compost heap
F   "Opal" plum
G   redcurrants (2x)
H   "Queen Victoria" plum
I   redcurrant (2x)
J   onion sets
K   gooseberries (5x)
M   cold frame
N   raspberries

1   red cabbage
2   garden peas, later endives
3   garden peas, later fennel

4   early beets, later Chinese beans
5   strawberries and lettuce
6   strawberries and lettuce
7   old potatoes
8   broad beans and new potatoes
9   peas, later French beans
10 chrysanthemum and winter carrots
11 oxheart cabbage, later curly kale
12 oxheart cabbage, later Brussels sprouts
13 chrysanthemums and celeriac
14 peas, later autumn leeks
15 broad beans and potatoes
16 strawberries and lettuce
17 carrots and onions
18 tomatoes
19 water tap point

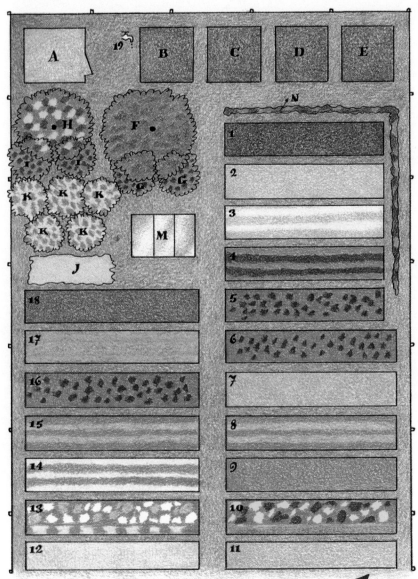

0   1   2   3m

A herb garden on a sandy soil

A good place to make a herb garden in the old kitchen garden was in front of the chicken coop. The old fruit trees have been kept, as has the border on the south-west side. A path of 30 x 30cm and 40 x 60cm concrete slabs runs behind the garage right across the herb garden, under the rose arch to the ornamental garden. Side paths ensure that the herbs can be reached in all weathers. A small pond with frogbit is slightly reminiscent of the well found in the herb gardens of bygone days. The edge of the pond is covered with turf, in which bugle, honesty and Filipendula hexapetala grow. Many old-fashioned, flowering plants can also be found here amongst the culinary herbs.

An overview of the herb garden shown on the plan.

Arrangement of plants in the herb garden on sandy soil:

1 *Althaea rosea* (hollyhock)

2 *Aconitum napellus* (monkshood)

3 *Anethum graveolens* (dill)

4 *Allium viviparum* (layered onion)

5 *Nepeta sibirica* (catmint)

6 *Artemisia ludoviciana* "Silver Queen"

7 *Melissa officinalis* (lemon balm)

8 *Santolina chamaecyparissias* (cotton lavender)

9 *Hyssopus officinalis* (hyssop)

10 *Salvia officinalis* (salvia)

11 *Origanum vulgare* (wild marjoram)

12 *Lavandula angustifolia* (lavender)

13 *Lysimachia nummularia* (Creeping Jenny) and *Ajuga reptans* (Bugle)

14 *Filipendula hexapetala* and *Lythrum salicaria* (purple loosestrife)

15 *Sanguisorba minor* (burnet)

16 *Allium schoenoprasum* (chives)

17 *Asperula odorata* (sweet woodruff)

18 *Matricaria recutita* (camomile)

19 *Thymus citriodorus* "Aureus" (lemon thyme)

20 *Digitalis purpurea* (foxglove)

138

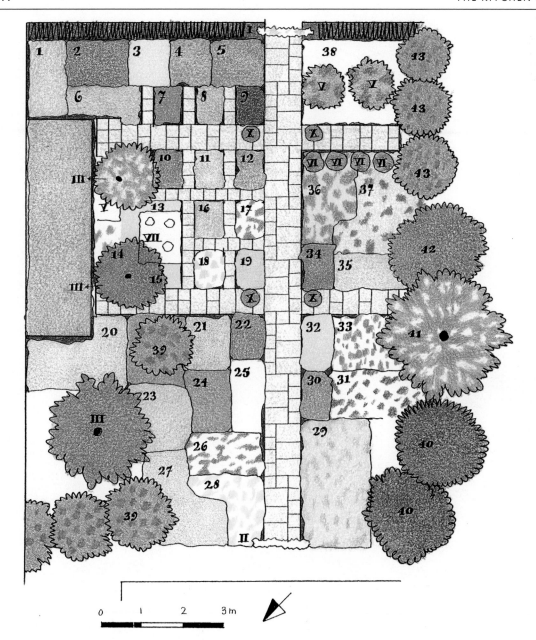

0   1   2   3 m

21 *Ruta graveolens* (rue)

22 *Satureja montana* (winter savoury)

23 *Levisticum officinale* (lovage)

24 *Lunaria annua* (Honesty)

25 *Pulmonaria officinalis* (lungwort)

26 *Tiarella cordifolia* (foam-flower)

27 *Campanula persicifolia* (peach-leaved bellflower)

28 *Myrrhis odorata* (Roman chervil)

29 *Angelica archangelica* (angelica)

30 *Apium graveolens* (celery)

31 *Campanula persicifolia* "Alba" (white peachleaved bellflower)

32 *Lysimachia nummularia* (loosestrife)

33 *Fragaria vesca* "Baron Somenacher"

34 *Petroselinum crispum* (parsley)

35 *Sanguisorba obtusa* (burnet)

36 *Alchemilla mollis* (lady's mantle)

37 *Monarda didyma* "Croftway Pink" (bergamot)

38 *Convallaria majalis* (lily of the valley)

39 *Ribes* (ornamental currant)

40 conifer

41 birch with *Clematis montana* Rubens over it

42 laurel

43 redcurrant

I   Rosa "New Dawn" over a rose arch

II Rosa "Mme Plantier" over a rose arch

III existing fruit trees

V   dwarf gooseberries

VI *Vaccinium murtillus* (bilberry, whortleberry)

X   *Buxus* in pots

Index

Acknowledgements

Photos: Lida Geers, Dongen, and Tjerk Buishand

The publisher and author would like to thank the following people and bodies for their valuable help in producing this book.

Mrs. A. Kemperman, Waarland; Mrs. T. v. d. Plank, Reeuwijk; Mrs. E. de Kieviet, Odijk; Mrs. H. van Wijhe, Rhenen; Mrs. C. Janssen, Klimmen; Mrs. M. Bulk, Ellewoutsdijk; Mrs. J. v. d. Stadt, Dedemsvaart; Mrs. E. Segers, Lochem.

Mr. B. Peeters, Dongen, Mr. A. Loonen, Dongen, Mrs. J. van der Heyden, Mrs. H. Bakx, Dongen; Organic kitchen gardening association "De Hovenier", Dongen; Mrs. J. Oomen, Bavel; Mrs. E. van Weede, Angerlo.

Sowing calendar granted for publication, Pieterpikzonen b.v. Heerenveen.

Bibliography

"Thuis in de moestuin" – "At home in the kitchen garden" produced by the horticultural teaching staff at the HVP and published by the Stichting Huishoudelijke en Consumentenvoorlichting HVP (Foundation for Household and Consumer Information), The Hague.

"Het nieuwe moestuinboek" – "The new kitchen garden book" by Wim Oudshoorn, Uitgeverij Zomer (Zomer Publishers) and Keuning Boeken BV, Ede

"Bijzondere oude en nieuwe groenten in tuin en keuken" – "Remarkable old and new vegetables in the garden and kitchen" by Tjerk Buishand/Harm P. Howing, Uitgeverij Terra (Terra Publishers), Zutphen.